A Taste of Class

Beverley Sutherland Smith

A Taste of Class

Beverley Sutherland Smith

Photographer Ray Joyce

SUMMIT BOOKS
Sydney. Auckland. London. New York.

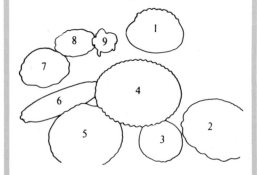

Half Title

Dessert Cake with Chocolate Cream and Straw-berries (page 152)

Title page

Duck with Sour Cherry Sauce (page 65)

INTRODUCTION

During the thirteen or so years that I have been teaching cooking, a collection of students, women and some men of all ages with disparate backgrounds, cooking ability and interests have attended lessons. Although each person has particular and differing tastes, some liking one recipe more than another, over the years there have emerged recipes which have proved to be the most useful and the most interesting. These have become much loved favourites and the aim of this book is to present these recipes.

When setting out a recipe I have included some of the different basic culinary principles which are used. For this reason sketches have been provided which will give extra assistance when preparing the dish.

At the end of each recipe you will find some extra notes: how long the dish keeps, alternative flavourings and anything else which may be helpful.

Because the school mainly teaches cooking for entertaining and special occasions some of the dishes are more expensive than others. For the same reason you will find that in the meat section, for example, there are very few recipes for minced meats, casseroles or stews. However, this does not mean that those included are all complicated or difficult; there are many recipes, first courses, vegetables, desserts and tarts which can be used every day.

Shortcuts should not be used. If there were any we would have discovered them during the testing of recipes. The dishes which may appear long are that way because any other method or recipe was nowhere as good as the one presented in this book.

When you have chosen a recipe that suits your particular purpose, be certain you have the correct ingredients, use the proper measurements and you will find that the recipe turns out perfectly. Not only have we tested recipes many times; students in the classes have also had success with these recipes, and this is the best testimonial of all.

There has been a tremendous upsurge of interest in cooking and entertaining. Cooking is fun, and cooking for friends is the most unselfish of all gifts.

This book is dedicated to my special four, Joanne, David, Suzanne and Scott

ACKNOWLEDGEMENTS

With special thanks to the girls who have worked with me, whose sense of humour and always-sharp knives have made our cooking in the school such a joy, Gwenda Bailey, Marie Stevens, Barbara Killeen, Sandra Cannington and Sue Macintosh.

The publishers would like to thank Pharoah's of Malvern, Ireland's Florist and Georges of Melbourne for providing the furniture, flowers and tableware and the family and friends of the author who kindly loaned items from their homes to enhance the photographs in this book.

Editor Ann Ferns, Designer Elaine Rushbrooke, Photographer Ray Joyce, Line drawing Michael White

Published by Summit Books
176 South Creek Road, Dee Why West, NSW, Australia 2099
First U.K. edition 1980
© Copyright Beverley Sutherland Smith 1980
Produced in Australia by the Publisher
Typeset in New Zealand by Jacobson Typesetters
Printed in Hong Kong
ISBN 0 7271 0503 5

CONTENTS

A NOTE BEFORE COOKING

Every recipe and the notes should be read before you put yourself in front of the stove. This only takes a couple of minutes and yet many people plunge forward without doing this. Recipes serve six unless otherwise indicated.

Knives should always be of a good quality and sharp as sharp as sharp.

The measurements in the book are metric as well as imperial. When a 'cup' is used then this means the official measuring cup, not the ordinary kitchen cup, which should never be used as it is not large enough.

In all the recipes which use chocolate I have used an eating chocolate rather than a cooking one. Melting of chocolate must be done very carefully so that the chocolate becomes light and fluid; overheating will cause it to firm into a sticky and lumpy mass.

To Heat Chocolate Place the chocolate in an enamel or china basin, stand this basin in a frying pan of water, and place the pan over a moderate heat. Stir the chocolate and keep the water in the pan hot but not boiling. Within a few minutes the chocolate will smooth out. If you want to melt chocolate with liquid you must use 2 tablespoons liquid for every 30 g (1 oz) of chocolate, which is quite a lot. Anything less than this and the chocolate will become firm and stiff instead of melting.

Butter In most of the recipes you may use either salted or unsalted butter. However, where it specifies unsalted butter this means it makes an important difference to the dish.

Flour Unless otherwise stated, flour used in the recipes is plain flour.

Eggs In all the recipes I have used large eggs (No. 65 grading), and if you use smaller ones you may need to adjust accordingly.

Gelatine Here is an ingredient which must be measured really accurately. A tablespoon means one that is shaken exactly level. The easiest way to dissolve gelatine is to place it in a cup, add cold water and stir so that the little dry bits at the base are mixed with the liquid. This sets almost immediately. Place the cup in a small saucepan, add water to the pan to come about halfway up the cup and place on the heat. Leave on the heat, stirring the gelatine once or twice, until it is clear. It can then be added to the dish.

Mushrooms Because most of the mushrooms you buy are grown under sterile conditions there is no need to wash them. Mushrooms absorb water rather like a sponge and when cooked, they release this water leaving a stewed mass in the pan. If you are concerned about the way they have been handled you can wipe the caps with some damp kitchen paper. The best flavour is in the skin and this should always be left on. If the stalks are a bit woody they can be removed and chopped very finely and used for soups or for dishes which have a longer cooking period.

Cultivated mushrooms are white or creamy on top. The underneath gills open up as they are kept in the shops and the caps spread out. If the tops and underneath are very dark and the caps have spread wide, then the mushrooms have been picked for some time; although still usable, when you cook them they will turn very dark in the dish.

Any mushroom which is blemished on top or slightly sweaty looking should never be used as it will have an unpleasant musty taste.

Parmesan cheese This is one cheese which needs to be freshly grated and for the recipes in this book it is best to grate your own. Although a large piece of parmesan is quite expensive, it keeps well if you wrap it loosely and place in a cool cupboard or in the refrigerator.

Shallots There are often misconceptions as to exactly what a shallot is. Smaller than an onion, with a golden brown skin, the cloves grow clustered together similiar to the way in which garlic grows. Spring onions are often substituted for shallots, but in reality their flavour is quite different.

If shallots are unobtainable, substitute 1 tablespoon finely chopped brown onion, mixed with ¼ clove of crushed garlic, for each shallot.

Whisks One of the most useful implements in the kitchen is the whisk. When mixing butter and flour for the base of the sauce use a wooden spoon, but once you add the liquid use a whisk and the sauce will always be smooth.

Savouries should not be considered as a course but rather as something to have with drinks before dinner. They should always be pleasing to the eye, tasty and interesting to the palate.

There are some various horrors which are still served, such as little bits of biscuit and toast garnished like a technicolor film with piping and titbits on top. I don't feel that this type of savoury fulfils any purpose at all and if you don't have the time to prepare something good then just serve some olives or nuts.

Most of the savouries in this section come more into the classification of 'finger foods'. They are especially good for cocktail parties because in general they are all prepared well in advance and are easy to serve.

SMOKED FISH CANÂPES

This savoury has a light smoked flavour. It is important to buy good quality smoked cod as some of the cheaper cod is very salted and rather too dry. Good fish will give a much more satisfactory result.

Place the fish and water in a frying pan. Place the 15 g (½ oz) piece of butter on top. Simmer gently for a short time, turning once, until tender. Remove and drain.

When cool, flake the fish with a fork, removing any bones and dark or tough pieces of skin.

Melt the 30 g (1 oz) butter in a small saucepan. Add the spring onions and sauté for a couple of minutes until they have just softened. Add the flour and stir to fry the flour in the butter for a moment but don't let it colour. Add the cream and stir until thick. This will thicken almost immediately because it is such a tiny amount of mixture. Remove from the heat immediately it thickens or it will turn oily. Add the pepper, mustard, Worcestershire sauce and the egg yolk.

Mix the sauce with the flaked fish.

Cover and refrigerate for 24 hours.

Fry the buttered circles of white or brown bread on both sides until crisp and golden.

To assemble

Spread some of the fish mixture on each circle of bread. Place on an unbuttered scone tray. Sprinkle a light coating of the parmesan cheese on top.

Bake in a moderate oven, 180-190°C (350-375°F) for approximately 8 minutes or until the mixture is hot and the top is golden in colour.

Note: The bread circles can be made ahead of the rest of the recipe and stored in an air-tight tin for up to two days.

Makes 24 savouries

INGREDIENTS
250 g (8 oz) smoked cod
2 cups (16 fl oz) water, approx.
15 g (½ oz) butter
30 g (1 oz) butter
2 tablespoons spring onion, diced
2 teaspoons flour
⅓ cup thick cream
pepper, use white or a pinch of cayenne
½ teaspoon dry, English-style mustard
½ teaspoon Worcestershire sauce
1 egg yolk
24 circles of white or brown bread, approximately 2.5 cm (1 in), buttered both sides
parmesan cheese, finely grated

MUSHROOM PATÉ

INGREDIENTS
30 g (1 oz) butter
1 medium-sized white onion, finely diced
1 rasher bacon, finely diced
250 g (8 oz) mushrooms
2 small tomatoes or 1 large ripe tomato,
*   peeled and cut into small pieces*
an extra 30 g (1 oz) butter
1 egg, beaten
salt and pepper
¼ teaspoon sugar

Jane Grigson is a very well-known English writer who has published many books, among them one on mushrooms. This excellent paté is one that she mentions in her book. The recipe originally appeared in a pamphlet which the Wine and Food Society of London published during the early 1940s. The original author of the recipe is unknown, the donor remained anonymous.

This paté keeps well for about 5 days and is nicest served on buttered toast or thin slices of buttered French bread.

Do not use the small white button mushrooms for this recipe as they don't have enough flavour, use mushrooms with the darker brown inside the cap.

Melt the butter in a saucepan and add the onions and bacon. Sauté until the onion is softened and the bacon fat transparent.

Wipe the mushrooms but do not wash or peel them as the best flavour is in the skin. Cut them into small dice. You can use the stalks if they are not too woody. Add the mushrooms to the pan with the tomatoes and the extra 30 g (1 oz) butter. Cook until the mixture is thick and all the vegetables are soft. The mixture should be rather dry looking, if not, turn up the heat, stir and cook to evaporate the liquid in the pan.

Put the mixture in a blender or through the coarse blade of a moulin. Return to the pan, add the beaten egg and cook, stirring for a few minutes until lightly thickened.

Season with the salt, pepper and sugar. The amount of salt used depends on the saltiness of the bacon.

As this is a cold spread, seasonings need to be fairly strong as chilling reduces flavourings.

Cover, chill, and keep refrigerated until ready to use.

Notes: This paté tastes delicious but does not look so attractive. You can garnish the top with a little parsley if you wish to brighten the presentation.

It is a good basic spread to keep as it has many uses apart from a savoury. It can be used to fill tomatoes or omelettes, or to spread on toast with a little grated cheese sprinkled over the top and then grilled. Or it can be warmed and used as an excellent topping for grilled steak.

STUFFED ENDIVE BELGIAN ENDIVE OR WHITLOF

When you buy endive select pieces which are pale cream or a light yellow on the end. Once the tips are greenish, endive is too strong and bitter.

Cut the base away from the endive and remove all the sections. Select some of the nicest centre ones and trim away any leafy part on the end. Place the strips of endive in some iced water to crisp them. Drain and pat dry.

Filling
Mash the cream cheese until soft, add anchovies and mash again. Season with pepper, add cream.

Using a piping bag and a star tube, pipe a strip down the stalk but leave a small end free. This makes the savoury much easier to hold.

Garnish
Turn the stuffed endive stalks over and press the top of the cheese gently onto the finely chopped spring onion. It sticks quite easily. Chill.

Notes: These can be prepared several hours before serving and are nicest if served really cold. The same recipe can be used with the nice, white inside stalks of celery.

If you are not keen on spring onions a little paprika can be sprinkled over the cream cheese.

There is no need to use salt in this recipe because anchovies are quite salty.

Makes 12 to 18 savouries, depending on the size of the endive pieces

INGREDIENTS
2 to 3 heads endive

FILLING
125 g (4 oz) cream cheese
1 x 45 g (1½ oz) tin flat anchovy fillets
a little white pepper
1 teaspoon cream

GARNISH
Finely chopped spring onion (use some of the green part of the onion as well as the white)

CHEESE BALLS WITH SESAME SEEDS

Mash the cream cheese with the blue cheese until soft. Season to taste with salt and pepper. (Seasoning varies according to the cheeses.) Add spring onions and mayonnaise. The mixture should be fairly smooth and soft.

Using a fork carefully mix the pink caviar through. Leave the mixture to chill as it will be too soft to handle. Place the sesame seeds either on a scone tray in the oven, or in a dry frying pan and heat until they are a light golden colour. Shake or stir them occasionally or they may not colour evenly. Leave the sesame seeds to cool.

When the cream cheese is firm, take teaspoons of the mixture and form into little balls. Next roll the balls around in the sesame seeds. Keep them chilled as they soften quickly.

They can be served plain or on a toothpick with a small piece of eating apple. Put the apple on the toothpick first, then add the cream cheese ball as it is difficult to pick them up otherwise.

Cheese Balls can be made about 12 hours beforehand but they should always be served directly from the refrigerator.

Makes 20 small savouries

INGREDIENTS
125 g (4 oz) cream cheese
1 tablespoon Danish blue or Roquefort cheese
salt and pepper
1 tablespoon spring onions, very finely diced
1 tablespoon mayonnaise
30 g (1 oz) pink caviar
sesame seeds (about ½ to ¾ cup) (3-5 oz)

CAVIAR PROFITEROLES

Makes 30 savouries

INGREDIENTS
CHOUX PASTRY
½ cup (4 fl oz) cold water
60 g (2 oz) butter, cut into small pieces
½ cup (2 oz) flour
¼ teaspoon salt
2 large eggs

FILLING
6 hard boiled eggs
salt and pepper
1 tablespoon finely grated white onion
2 tablespoons well flavoured mayonnaise
3 teaspoons finely chopped parsley
sour cream for topping
1 x 45 g (1½ oz) jar red or black caviar

This savoury is based on tiny little choux puffs filled with egg and topped with caviar. The recipe makes about 30 profiteroles. However, you can halve the quantity of filling and freeze the remaining puffs for another time. Before using them, thaw for about 4 to 5 minutes in a moderately hot oven 200° C (400° F). Place the cold water in a saucepan. Add the butter. Bring to the boil and make certain that the butter is fully melted by the time the water boils. Sift the flour and salt onto a piece of paper.

Remove the pan from the heat and add the flour all at once. Stir well, return to the heat. Cook until it leaves the sides of the saucepan and begins to film the base of the saucepan which usually takes only a minute. Leave to cool for a couple of minutes.

Beat the eggs with a fork and then add gradually to the pastry, beating well. You can do this by hand or use a mixer or food processor. It takes much longer by hand but if you beat well with a wooden spoon for a few minutes they will mix in perfectly. Sometimes you don't need to add all the egg. The mixture should hold a shape when lifted with a spoon.

Grease a baking tray with butter. Put the mixture into a pastry bag with a large plain tube and pipe small portions out about the size of a 20 cent piece. Or you can place small teaspoons of the mixture on the tray.

If there is any egg left over mix it with a teaspoon of milk and brush the top of the puffs with this to glaze them. Otherwise use another egg.

Bake the puffs in a moderately hot oven 200° C (400° F) for about 20 minutes, then turn the oven down to moderate, 180° C (350° F) and leave them for another 5 to 10 minutes. When they are cooked and crisp, remove from the tray and pierce the side of each one to release the steam, otherwise they will soften. Turn off your oven, leave the door open and leave them to dry and cool for 10 minutes.

They can be kept in an airtight tin for days, or even a week. If they have softened at all, just place them back in the oven for a few minutes and they will become crisp again.

Mash the hard boiled eggs with salt, pepper, onion, mayonnaise and parsley. The mixture should·be moist and well seasoned.

Cut the top from each choux puff. Using a teaspoon or coffee spoon fill them with the egg mixture, mounding it just slightly. Place a little dob of sour cream on the top and then some caviar.

You can fill the puffs about 30 minutes before serving them but no sooner or they will soften.

Notes: Ideally the caviar is added almost at the last moment, especially if you use black caviar, as the colouring makes the sour cream a strange grey colour.

If you want to make a rather stunning platter, use both red and black caviar. Serve the puffs together on a tray, with black caviar puffs on one side and red puffs on the other side.

As an alternative to caviar a little smoked salmon can be placed on top of the profiteroles.

SPICED FILLET ROLLS

Trim the fillet steak well. Cover with plastic wrap and freeze until it is very firm. This makes it much easier to cut. Timing for freezing will vary between 1 hour and 1 hour 15 minutes.

Cut the fillet into thin slices with a very sharp knife. Leave to thaw. This only takes about a minute. Using a large flat knife, press each slice firmly on top to flatten a little.

Filling

Mix all the ingredients together until smooth and creamy. Spread a very thin layer of filling on each piece of fillet. Roll up tightly and secure with a toothpick. If very large, each roll can be cut into two sections.

Place rolls on a buttered tray and cook under a griller, turning once until brown and just cooked through. This will only take about a minute because they are so thin. Do not overcook.

Sauce

Dice any large pieces in the chutney. Add a little salt, pepper and the cream. Keep refrigerated.

Dip the fillet rolls in this just before eating.

Notes: These rolls can be prepared in the morning, covered with plastic wrap and then refrigerated. Remove them about 30 minutes before cooking so that the meat will be at room temperature. You can put different types of fillings in the beef, for example French mustard or chutney which are simple but good.

Makes approximately 24 small rolls

INGREDIENTS
250 g (8 oz) fillet steak

FILLING
1 tablespoon crunchy peanut butter
2 teaspoons soy sauce
1 teaspoon brown sugar
few drops Tabasco sauce
good pinch salt
good pinch pepper
2 teaspoons lemon juice
1 teaspoon white vinegar

SAUCE
1 tablespoon mango chutney, medium hot
salt and pepper
2 tablespoons cream, lightly whipped

BACON ROLLS WITH SARDINE FILLING

Drain the oil from the sardines and mash them with a fork. Melt the butter and sauté the onion until softened, not brown.

Add the onion, mayonnaise, black pepper, Worcestershire sauce and breadcrumbs. The mixture should be moist but not too wet. If it is too moist add a few more crumbs.

Place the bacon flat on the bench. Put a teaspoon of the filling on one end. Roll over to enclose the filling and cut across. Secure the edge with a toothpick. Use up all the filling and if the rolls are too wide, cut them into halves.

Place on an ungreased scone tray. (There is no need to grease the tray as the bacon has sufficient fat.)

Bake in moderate oven 180-190° C (350-375° F) for about 10 minutes or until the bacon is cooked.

Cut some buttered toast into pieces, just big enough to fit under the bacon rolls. Remove the toothpicks and place one on each piece of toast.

These can be prepared during the day but once they are cooked should be eaten immediately.

Note: For the best result try to buy bacon that is not too fatty.

This makes approximately 16 to 20 bacon rolls

INGREDIENTS
1 x 120 g (4 oz) tin sardines
45 g (1½ oz) butter
1 white onion, finely diced
2 teaspoons mayonnaise
black pepper
2 teaspoons Worcestershire sauce
2 tablespoons breadcrumbs
4 to 5 full rashers of bacon, rind removed
1 small square of toast for each bacon roll
toothpicks

ANCHOVY AND EGG PUFFS

Makes 40 tiny savouries; 20 larger puffs

INGREDIENTS
1 hard boiled egg
1 x 45 g (1½ oz) tin flat anchovy fillets
1 tablespoon parsley, finely chopped
1 clove garlic, crushed
1 tablespoon grated onion, with any juice
black pepper
½ cup ham, finely minced
500 g (1 lb) puff pastry
1 small egg, lightly beaten

Mash the egg and mix in the anchovies, mashing with a fork to mix them thoroughly. Add the parsley, garlic, onion, pepper and ham and mash together well.

Roll out the puff pastry until it is thin. Cut into circles about 5 cm (2 in) for the small puffs or 8 cm (3 in) for large puffs.

Place a small spoonful of the egg mixture on one side of the circle. Fold over and shape until it is like a little pasty. Pinch the edges together and check that there are no gaps.

Brush the edges of the pastry with egg, then brush over the top. Prick once or twice in the centre. Chill.

Place the puffs on a lightly buttered scone or oven tray with shallow sides. Bake in a hot oven 220° C (425° F) for about 15 minutes or until the pastry is golden and the savoury is puffed.

Notes: These can be made and refrigerated for 24 hours before baking. They can also be cooked beforehand and then reheated but are at their best when cooked just once.

Quite often, brushing the edges of puff pastry with egg to seal them makes it rather slippery. As these puffs are tiny, they become very difficult to handle. It is just as satisfactory to join the dry edges and then brush with egg afterwards.

The tiny savouries are very fiddly to make, but look very nice. I have found that the larger puffs are much easier to make.

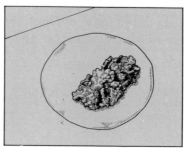 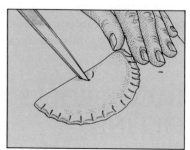

1. Place a small spoonful of the filling on one side of the puff pastry circles. *2. Fold over to enclose and pinch the edges together firmly.*

MINIATURE MUSHROOM CRÊPES

Makes approximately 24

INGREDIENTS
CRÊPE MIXTURE
4 tablespoons flour
pinch salt
1 egg
1 egg yolk
1 cup milk
1 tablespoon vegetable oil

These are tiny crêpes which are folded in half, with a creamy mushroom filling and then gently fried in butter so that the outside becomes just barely crisp. They need to be small enough to be just a mouthful, or at the most two bites, otherwise they are messy to eat.

Crêpes
Sift the flour and salt into a large mixing bowl and make a well in the centre. Add the egg, egg yolk and a few spoons of the milk. Stir around so the flour is gradually incorporated into the centre. Then add enough milk to make the mixture the consistency of a light cream. Add the oil.

Leave to stand at room temperature for about 1 hour. The

mixture will thicken up during this time, and before using it add extra milk to thin it down again.

Before making the crêpes set aside half cup of the batter. This will be used to finish the dish and if you do not do it first it is easy to forget and make up the full quantity into crêpes.

Heat a flat frying pan and add a tiny piece of butter, tilting until it covers the bottom with a thin film. Take a dessertspoon of the batter and let it fall from the end of the spoon so it forms a tiny miniature crêpe, about 5 cm (2 in) across. Do not worry if they are ragged and uneven around the edge as they can easily be trimmed later. The important thing is to make them very thin.

Pile them up on a plate and they will not dry out.

Filling

Melt the butter and cook the onion gently until softened but do not let it brown. Turn up the heat, add the mushrooms, seasoning with salt, pepper and the lemon juice. By cooking over rapid heat you do not stew them and should not have any moisture in the pan. Cook until just softened, remove immediately and add the garlic.

Place the filling in a small bowl and stir in the sour cream, parsley and parmesan cheese. Leave it to cool before using.

To Assemble

In each crêpe place a teaspoon of the mushroom filling on one side. Fold in half. Using a pastry brush, brush the outside of each crêpe with the extra batter and dab a little on the centre join. This will seal them completely.

Dip in crumbs, pressing down gently.

To Cook

Melt a tiny piece of butter with a couple of teaspoons of oil in a large frying pan. When it is foaming, add the tiny crêpes, a few at a time and cook, turning once, until they are just slightly crisp on the outside.

Drain them on paper towelling and keep warm in a low oven until they are all cooked. Don't keep them in the oven too long though or they may become soggy.

Arrange them on a platter and dust the top lightly with the extra grated parmesan cheese.

Notes: These are rather time consuming but for a special occasion they are well worth the effort. They can be completely finished, right up to the dipping in the crumbs, then kept 24 hours, covered with plastic wrap in the refrigerator.

A variety of fillings could be used instead of the mushrooms as long as it is a filling which has plenty of flavour. For example you could use finely chopped cooked spinach, minced crayfish, minced smoked clams or minced ham.

Although parmesan cheese can be bought grated, it becomes strong and sour in taste if it is kept for long. It is much better to buy the parmesan in a piece and grate it as you need it.

MUSHROOM FILLING
30 g (1 oz) butter
1 white onion, finely diced
125 g (4 oz) mushrooms, finely chopped
salt and pepper
squeeze lemon juice
1 clove garlic, crushed
1 tablespoon sour cream
1 tablespoon parsley, finely chopped
1 tablespoon parmesan cheese, freshly grated

TO ASSEMBLE
½ cup (4 fl oz) crêpe batter
breadcrumbs from stale bread
butter
oil
small quantity parmesan cheese, grated

CHICKEN WINGS MARIPOSA

INGREDIENTS
24 chicken wings, prepared

MARINADE
½ cup (4 fl oz) soy sauce
½ cup (4 fl oz) white vinegar
2 teaspoons chilli sauce
½ cup (4 fl oz) tomato sauce
¼ cup (2½ oz) light brown sugar
¼ cup (2½ oz) honey
1 tablespoon Hoi Sin Paste
2 cloves garlic, crushed
*1 small piece (about 2.5 cm (1 in)) green
ginger, peeled and grated*

For many years the sister ships, *Mariposa* and *Monterey* plied between the United States and Australia, carrying groups of mostly elderly, mostly very wealthy people who found the shipboard holiday almost a way of life.

Food, morning, noon and night was an integral part of shipboard existence and a very popular tradition was the glamorous cocktail hour before dinner with a generous selection of hot and cold savouries. These two ships were the last of the American first-class passenger liners but before the kitchens closed for the last time, I was given a collection of recipes. This one, Chicken Wings Mariposa, was one of the most delicious and popular savouries on board. The marinade is simple to do but the actual handling of the chicken wings is a little more involved but worth the effort.

Preparation of Chicken Wings

The first time I prepared these, each one took several minutes to trim. However, after doing several, one picks up speed, so do not be discouraged if you seem to be going very slowly at first. I must admit, though, I only prepare this dish for special friends.

Wash the chicken wings. Cut off the wing tips at the joint as in this dish it is only the first joint that is used. The remaining parts of the wings can be put in a pot to make stock, or they can be cooked and served for a snack another time.

Hold the small end of the bone. Using a tiny knife, cut directly towards the bone to sever the tendons and cut through the skin. Then scrape the flesh down the bone until it is all down at one end. Using your fingers pull the skin and meat over the bone, turning it inside out. The wing now looks like a baby drumstick. Remove any untidy bits of skin on the bone.

You can prepare the chicken wings the day before you want to marinate them, provided you keep them covered and stored in the refrigerator.

Marinade

Mix all the ingredients together and place in a china or glass bowl. Add the prepared chicken wings and leave to marinate for 2 hours. If you do not want to cook them immediately, remove and place on a plate. Keep covered and refrigerated. Do not leave them in the marinade for too long or the taste will be too strong.

The marinade can be used again. It keeps for about 4 days if stored in the refrigerator.

To cook

Remove the chicken wings from the marinade. Grease the base of a baking dish with a little oil. Arrange the chicken wings on top. Add about half a cup (4 fl oz) of the marinade to the pan. Bake in a moderate oven 180-190° C (350-375° F) for about 20 to 25 minutes or until tender. You need to baste them once or twice with the marinade in the baking tin and watch that the marinade doesn't cook away or it will caramelise and burn very easily. If the pan is becoming too dry add a little extra marinade.

When the wings are cooked, remove from the oven and spoon the liquid over the top once or twice.

They can be served immediately or else you can prepare them beforehand, wrap loosely in foil and reheat for about 10 minutes in the oven.

You need lots of paper serviettes with these because they are rather sticky from the marinade.

Note: This particular marinade could also be used for chicken portions, using the same method.

1. Remove tips and sever wings at the joint. Use only the portions which were attached to the breast.

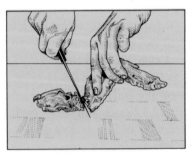

2. Hold firmly at the joint and cut the wing directly towards the bone to sever the tendons.

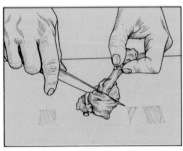

3. Scrape the flesh down towards the bone until it is at one end.

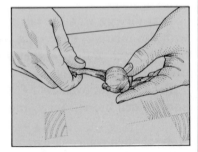

4. Using fingers, turn the flesh inside out to form a small ball of meat.

HAM CRESCENTS

Makes 16 to 20 small crescents

INGREDIENTS

FILLING

125 g (4 oz) ham
30 g (1 oz) butter
1 medium-sized white onion, finely diced
1 clove garlic, crushed
1 tablespoon sweet sherry
pinch cayenne pepper
½ teaspoon dry, English-style mustard
1 teaspoon flour
¼ cup (2 fl oz) chicken stock
1 tablespoon cream

PASTRY

250 g (8 oz) puff pastry
1 egg
pinch salt
butter for greasing

These are tiny crescents made with puff pastry and filled with ham. Because of their size they make a perfect little savoury to serve with drinks. However, you can make larger ones and serve as an accompaniment for soup.

Put the ham through a mincer. Melt the butter and add onion and garlic. Cook gently until softened but be careful not to let them brown.

Add the ham, sweet sherry, cayenne and mustard. Sprinkle the flour over the top and stir thoroughly until not a trace of flour is visible in the mixture.

Immediately add the stock and cream and stir until it comes to the boil. The mixture will be very liquid and you must cook this until there is no moisture left in the pan, otherwise the filling will not be firm enough to roll inside the pastry.

Leave aside to cool.

Roll the puff pastry out thinly. Cut into squares approximately 10-12.5 cm (4-5 in). Cut each square into 2 triangles. Pick up a triangle and place down with the wide side nearest to you. Using a teaspoon or a coffee spoon spread a little of the ham filling along the wide side. Roll over from wide side, tucking the filling under as you go. The ends sometimes look a little ragged but you can just tuck them in if this happens. Bend gently to form a crescent shape.

Beat the egg with the salt and brush the top of the crescents with this mixture. Place on a buttered scone tray, leaving space between each of them as they will puff up as they cook. Chill 30 minutes before baking.

Bake in a hot oven 200° C (425° F) for about 15 minutes or until golden brown. Serve immediately.

Notes: When you cook ham it becomes saltier, do not season the filling with any salt. If possible use a very undersalted stock when adding to the filling, and if your stock is too highly seasoned, break it down with a little water.

Although these are best made with minced ham, if you do not have a mincer then buy 125 g (4 oz) of very thinly sliced ham. You can then dice this very, very finely and use in the recipe.

The crescents can be made 24 hours beforehand and kept refrigerated, but are nicest if cooked only once and served fresh.

Caviar Profiteroles (page 12)

1. Roll over, tucking the filling under.   *2. Form a crescent.*

SOUPS

Despite the fact that the shelves of the supermarkets feature a large variety of tinned and packaged soups there just isn't any comparison with the fresh flavour that you get when you make soup yourself.

I have especially chosen a few unusual soups, such as the Leek and Pear, and the Tomato, Cucumber and Avocado, as well as a couple of more traditional recipes. All these soups should give an interesting start to a dinner.

SIMPLE CHICKEN STOCK

Rather than using chicken giblets we usually make our stock from chicken livers. This stock has a clear and golden colour and has lots of flavour. It rarely has any fat on the top. This simple stock can be used in any of the recipes which require stock. It will keep for about 5 days in the refrigerator or it can be kept frozen. It is always better to undersalt stock as many of the recipes require cooking to reduce or strengthen flavour and this also of course makes the finished stock saltier. This is no problem if you use undersalted stock as it is easy to adjust the seasoning in the finished dish later.

Check the livers to see that they are free from any green, and remove these sections if you should find any. Place the livers into a pan and add the water and salt. Bring slowly to the boil. During this time a certain amount of brown scum will form on the top and you should remove this with a spoon. When the top is clear, cover and cook gently for about 1½ hours.

Remove the pan from the heat and leave to settle for about 10 minutes and then strain. This stock sometimes contains little specks from the livers; if you want really clear stock you can strain it through a piece of cheesecloth but in most dishes where the stock is mixed with other ingredients for a sauce this is not really necessary.

INGREDIENTS
500 g (1 lb) chicken livers
4 cups (1½ pints) water
¼ teaspoon salt

Leek and Pear Soup (page 22)

21

CLAM CHOWDER

INGREDIENTS

1 x 290 g (10 oz) tin clams
60 g (2 oz) butter
1 medium-sized white onion, finely diced
2 rashers of bacon, finely diced
*1 medium-sized green pepper, seeds
 removed, diced*
1 cup (8 fl oz) water
½ teaspoon salt
white pepper
1 cup (4 oz) diced potato
2 cups (16 fl oz) milk

GARNISH
2 tablespoons parsley, finely chopped

There is a great deal of dissension regarding this favourite American soup. One of the varieties is a pale, creamy coloured soup, and is supposedly the authentic New England chowder; another is made with tomatoes and becomes pink in colour. This is named 'Manhattan Clam Chowder'.

This recipe is more like the New England version, but slightly altered as tinned clams are used. Tinned clams can be bought at most large supermarkets and the flavour is very good.

Drain the clams and place them aside but be sure to keep the liquid as this is used in the soup. Melt the butter in a saucepan, add the onion, bacon and pepper.

Cook gently over fairly low heat stirring occasionally, until the onion is softened and the bacon fat is transparent. Add the clam liquid, water, salt and pepper and diced potato. Cover the saucepan and cook gently until the potato pieces are quite tender. Add the milk and clams and heat through. Once the milk is added do not boil as the soup will curdle and look unpleasant. Although it still tastes quite good the appearance of the soup is spoilt.

Check seasoning and garnish with parsley.

Notes: This soup has a delicate fishy flavour and improves by being made 24 hours beforehand and then refrigerated. Prepare completely but do not garnish with the parsley until you are ready to serve.

The vegetables can be varied, although always use the onion, bacon and pepper. Drained kernels of sweet corn can be added and also a finely diced carrot can be added at the same time as the potato pieces.

LEEK AND PEAR SOUP

INGREDIENTS
60 g (2 oz) butter
*1 bunch leeks, thinly sliced (use a little of
 the green part)*
500 g (1 lb) green pears
4 cups (1½ pints) chicken stock
salt and pepper

This is a rather unusual and very delicate soup, the taste has just a trace of fruit. I have found that it is important to use fairly firm, green pears otherwise the sugar which develops in ripe pears makes the soup a little sweet.

Melt the butter in a saucepan and add the leeks. Sauté, stirring occasionally until they have softened but do not let them brown.

Peel and core the pears and cut either into rough dice or slices. Add the pears to the pan and cook for a few minutes. Add chicken stock, bring to the boil, cover the pan and simmer gently until the pears are quite soft. The timing varies, it may take from 20 minutes to 45 minutes.

Put the mixture through a moulin or sieve. Add salt and pepper to taste.

If you find the soup is sweet add a little lemon juice.

Note: This soup keeps for several days. It can be served plain or garnished with a spoonful of cream before serving.

MIXED SHELLFISH SOUP

This is one of the most beautiful of all the luxury fish soups. Follow the directions carefully as it spoils if the various shellfish are overcooked.

Clean the scallops, keep the coral. Place the oysters in a small bowl, keeping any of the liquid around them. Shell the prawns and cut into small pieces.

Place the scallops in the cup of milk and leave to stand for several hours. Drain but be careful to keep the milk as this is used in the sauce. If the scallops are really large they can be cut in halves across the grain.

Court Bouillon

Place all the ingredients in a saucepan and bring to the boil. Cover and simmer gently for about 30 minutes. Pour through a strainer and press down gently with a spoon to extract most of the flavour from the vegetables.

The Soup

Melt the butter and add the flour. Cook, stirring for a few minutes until the flour is granulated and dry, but do not allow it to brown.

Add the Court Bouillon, stir continuously until the mixture boils and thickens lightly. Add the milk and reheat.

Add the scallops, prawns and oysters. Once the milk and seafood are added do not boil the soup; it can now be kept hot for a few minutes during which time the scallops will cook. They take only a short time to cook through and by adding them raw you gain the maximum flavour.

Mix the cream and egg yolks together in a small basin. Add a little of the hot soup to the basin, stir, return to the saucepan and stir for a minute to heat. The egg yolks will thicken the soup slightly. Check for seasoning. Before serving add the garnish.

Garnish

Peel the carrot. Cut into long strips and then cut these into long, thin slivers, about the size of a matchstick. Place them in a saucepan and cover with water. Season with a little salt and cook uncovered until they are just tender. This should only take a few minutes. Drain and leave aside.

Cut the mushroom stalks level with the caps. Cut mushrooms into thin slices and leave aside. The mushrooms are not cooked at all beforehand as they will cook through almost instantly when they are placed in the soup and this way remain white and firm when served. A garnish of carrot, mushroom and parsley is added at the end. If the soup is made beforehand and reheated, leave the garnish until the soup is reheated and ready to serve.

Note: The soup improves by being made some time beforehand. If you make it in the morning for a dinner at night, refrigerate as soon as it is cool. Reheat gently, giving it an occasional stir. It will keep for 24 hours.

INGREDIENTS

SHELLFISH MIXTURE
500 g (1 lb) scallops
1 dozen oysters
250 g (8 oz) prawns
1 cup (8 fl o) milk

THE COURT BOUILLON
2 white onions, roughly diced
1 medium-sized carrot, finely diced
pinch thyme
few peppercorns
clove garlic, cut in half
1 tea poon salt
½ bay leaf
2 cups (16 fl oz) water
2 cups (16 fl oz) dry white wine

THE SOUP BASE
30 g (1 oz) butter
2 tablespoons flour
the Court Bouillon
the milk in which the scallops are soaked
½ cup (4 fl oz) cream
2 egg yolks

GARNISH
1 medium-sized carrot
water
salt
5 medium-sized mushrooms, about 125 g (4 oz)
1 tablespoon parsley, finely chopped

CUCUMBER SOUP

INGREDIENTS
60 g (2 oz) butter (if serving the soup hot)
*2 tablespoons light vegetable oil (if serving
    the soup cold)*
2 medium-sized white onions, finely diced
1⅔ cucumbers
1 tablespoon flour
2 cups (16 fl oz) chicken stock
1 clove garlic, crushed
¾ cup (6 fl oz) cream

GARNISH
⅓ cucumber
salt
a little sugar
½ cup (4 fl oz) cream, lightly whipped
parsley or chives, finely chopped

This lightly flavoured soup is equally delicious hot or cold.

Melt the butter (or oil) in a saucepan. Add the onion and sauté for a minute.

Peel the cucumbers. Cut about a third off one and place aside; this will be used as the garnish later. Cut the remainder into thin slices or dice. Add to the pan and sauté with the onions until slightly softened, which usually takes about 10 to 15 minutes. Add the flour and fry for a few minutes stirring continuously.

Add chicken stock and bring to the boil, stirring continuously. Cover the pan, and simmer for about 25 minutes or until the cucumber is quite soft. Put through a moulin. Return to the pan to reheat, add the garlic and cream. Check seasoning.

To Garnish
Cut the cucumber piece into halves lengthwise. Using a small teaspoon, scoop out the seeds. Cut the flesh into thin slices. Place these in a shallow bowl and sprinkle with a little salt and a little sugar.

Leave to stand for about 30 minutes. Drain and pat dry.

To Serve Hot
Heat the soup and add the extra cucumber. Cook for about 3 or 4 minutes to soften the cucumber slightly.

Ladle into soup bowls with a little spoonful of cream on top and garnish with parsley or chives.

To Serve Cold
After making the soup leave it to cool, uncovered, giving it an occasional stir.

It will need plenty of seasoning once it is cooled. Cover and refrigerate until you are ready to serve.

When serving, place into soup bowls, add the raw cucumber to the top and then place a little spoonful of cream over this. Top with parsley or chives.

Note: When making soup to be served chilled, you must be careful that the stock used does not have a trace of fat on top otherwise the soup will be greasy.

CURRIED LAMB SOUP

This is a hot spicy soup which is suitable for a cold evening. If you find it a little hot you can cut back slightly on the amount of curry powder used. Curry powders vary in heat and I generally make this with a Madras curry powder which is only moderately hot. The soup keeps well for days and in fact is much improved in flavour by being made 24 hours before eating.

Melt the butter in a saucepan and add the apple and onion. Sauté gently until slightly softened. Dice the meat into small pieces, removing as much fat as possible.

Add the meat to the pan, turn up the heat and fry, stirring until the meat has changed colour. Add the garlic, curry powder and flour and continue stirring, otherwise they will stick. Add the chicken stock, bring to the boil and then cover and cook gently until the meat is tender. This may take from 30 to 45 minutes depending on the cut of lamb.

Bring a small saucepan of water to the boil, add a little salt and 2 tablespoons of rice. Cook over high heat until the rice is just tender. Drain and add to the soup when the meat is cooked.

Garnish

Peel the tomato. Cut into quarters and squeeze out the seeds. Cut the quarters of tomato into thin strips. Leave aside.

Add the mango chutney to the whipped cream. If there are large chunks of fruits in the chutney, cut these into tiny pieces.

To Serve

Add the tomato strips to the soup for 1 minute to heat them through. Pour some of the soup into each soup bowl. Top with a spoonful of the cream and chutney mixture.

Notes: When buying the lamb for this, it is just as easy to ask for some large leg chops. The fat can be quickly trimmed and they are easily boned. They also cook fairly quickly. If you prefer, this soup can also be made using chicken instead of lamb.

INGREDIENTS

60 g (2 oz) butter
1 medium-sized green apple, peeled and diced
2 medium-sized white onions, finely diced
250 g (8 oz) lean lamb
1 clove garlic, crushed
1 tablespoon curry powder
1 tablespoon flour
4 cups (1½ pints) chicken stock
water
salt
2 tablespoons rice

GARNISH

1 ripe tomato
1 tablespoon medium hot mango chutney
½ cup (4 fl oz) cream, whipped

CREAM OF EGGPLANT SOUP

This soup has a lovely flavour but doesn't look particularly attractive, so you can garnish if you wish with a little diced tomato or some chopped chives to add colour.

Dice the eggplant but do not peel. Sprinkle a little salt over the eggplant and leave to stand for about 30 minutes. Put in a strainer and run a little water over the dice, pat dry. This removes any bitter taste which would spoil the soup.

Melt the butter in a saucepan and add the onion, celery and eggplant. Sauté, stirring occasionally until the vegetables have slightly softened. Eggplant absorbs butter very rapidly so you may have to add a little more or the vegetables will stick.

Add the curry powder and fry to release the flavours. Add thyme, basil, chicken stock and the potato. Cover and simmer until the vegetables are quite soft, about 30 minutes.

Put the soup through a sieve or moulin and add the cream. Taste for seasoning.

Notes: This soup keeps well for several days. However, if you intend making it beforehand and keeping it only add the cream when you reheat it. It thickens as it stands, but it can be thinned with a little milk.

INGREDIENTS

500 g (1 lb) eggplant
salt
60 g (2 oz) butter
1 medium-sized white onion, finely diced
2 stalks celery, diced
1 teaspoon curry powder
pinch thyme
pinch basil
4 cups (1½ pints) chicken stock
1 cup (4 oz) potato, diced
½ cup (4 fl oz) cream
salt and pepper

PARSNIP AND ORANGE SOUP

INGREDIENTS
500 g (1 lb) parsnips
60 g (2 oz) butter
1 white onion, finely diced
½ teaspoon curry powder
3 cups (1¼ pints) chicken or veal stock
rind of 1 orange, grated
3 tablespoons orange juice
salt and pepper to taste

The parsnips give only a light flavour to this soup. It does have a slight trace of sweetness but the orange helps to freshen the flavour. It keeps well for several days.

Peel the parsnips and cut into halves lengthwise. Remove any hard or woody parts. Cut into slices or dice them.

Melt the butter in a saucepan and add the parsnips and onion. Sauté gently until they are glazed and slightly softened. Stir occasionally as parsnip has a tendency to stick.

Add the curry powder and leave to fry for a moment, then toss vegetables through to coat them. Add stock and orange rind, cover the saucepan and cook gently until the parsnips are quite soft. This usually takes about 25 minutes but it depends on how large they are.

Remove from the heat, add the orange juice. Put the soup through a moulin or blender. Reheat and check for seasoning.

WATERCRESS SOUP

INGREDIENTS
60 g (2 oz) butter
2 medium-sized white onions, finely diced
1 leek, well washed and finely chopped (use just a little of the green part at the top)
6 cups (2½ pints) chicken or veal stock
1 cup (4 oz) potato, peeled and cut into small dice
1 bunch watercress
½ cup (4 oz) cream
salt and pepper to taste

Fresh watercress gives this creamy soup a slight spiciness. Unfortunately very few local greengrocers or shops bother to keep watercress even when it is in season, however local markets will nearly always have plenty. It is very cheap to buy but make sure that it is green and not yellowing or very pale. Use watercress within 24 hours of purchase.

This soup keeps well for several days.

Melt the butter in a large saucepan. Add the onions and leek. Sauté gently, stirring occasionally until the vegetables are softened but not browned.

Add the stock and the diced potatoes. Bring to the boil and cover the pan. Simmer gently until the potatoes are quite soft.

In the meantime, wash the watercress well. Remove any very bruised leaves or stalks which are very thick and woody. Pull or cut away most of the leaves and then cut the stalk part into rough pieces. Add the stalks to the soup first and cook them until tender. The time can vary; usually about 10 minutes is long enough. Then, add the leaves of the watercress and cook another 1 minute.

Put the soup through a fine moulin or sieve. Reheat and add the cream and salt and pepper to taste. The potatoes will slightly thicken the soup, and if you find it a little too thick, thin down with milk.

Notes: Watercress soup can be served hot or cold. If you wish to serve it chilled, instead of using the butter to sauté the vegetables, place them in the saucepan and simmer with the stock. Be very careful to use stock that is absolutely free from any trace of fat when making a cold soup. It usually needs to be seasoned very well as chilled soup loses flavour. Thin with milk until it is the right consistency.

GREEN TOMATO SOUP

This tomato soup is a little unusual in that although the tomatoes should not be really hard and bright green, under-ripened tomatoes are used. Or, if you cannot get all under-ripe ones, use some red tomatoes and some green ones. This soup has a slightly tart but refreshing flavour. Tomato paste is added mainly for additional colour, otherwise the soup is a rather uninteresting, pale shade.

Cut the tomatoes into rough pieces. Melt the butter in a saucepan and add the onions. Cook until slightly softened but do not let them brown. Add the tomatoes and garlic and cook for about 10 minutes, giving it an occasional stir until the tomatoes have started to soften.

Add the peppercorns, sugar, bay leaf and tomato paste. Cover and cook until the tomatoes are soft. The time varies, probably about 15 to 20 minutes should be enough.

Add the chicken stock, bring to the boil, cover and cook for another 15 minutes.

Push through a sieve or moulin but do not blend this soup. Check whether the soup requires additional salt, pepper or sugar to your taste.

Garnish

Place the ham flat on a board and cut it into thin strips about the size of a matchstick. Add these to the hot soup, cook 30 seconds only, just enough to heat the ham and sprinkle each serving with a little parsley.

Notes: The soup keeps for about 3 days refrigerated. Instead of the ham and parsley a garnish of a little finely chopped mint goes well with the tartness of this soup.

Although a tablespoon of sugar may seem a lot I usually find it too acidic without this; however if you are doubtful about the amount, which does depend on the season for tomatoes, add less sugar at first and then season after the soup is cooked.

INGREDIENTS

1 kg (2 lb) slightly green and firm
  tomatoes
60 g (2 oz) butter
2 medium-sized white onions, finely diced
1 clove garlic, crushed
6 peppercorns
1 tablespoon sugar
½ bay leaf
1 tablespoon tomato paste
3 cups chicken stock
salt and pepper

GARNISH

60 g (2 oz) ham slices
1 tablespoon parsley, finely chopped

CHICKEN AND APPLE SOUP

INGREDIENTS

30 g (1 oz) butter

1 medium-sized clove garlic, crushed

2 teaspoons tomato paste

2 tablespoons flour

4 cups (1½ cups) chicken stock

an additional 30 g (1 oz) butter

1 green apple, about 185 g (6 oz), peeled and diced

¼ teaspoon sugar

½ teaspoon curry powder

½ cup (4 fl oz) cream

4 to 5 spring onions, very finely chopped

salt and pepper to taste

Although the ingredients are basically simple the finished soup is quite exotic and has an unusual flavour.

Melt the butter. Add the garlic and tomato paste and stir for about 30 seconds. Add flour and fry for a couple of minutes. Add the chicken stock and bring to the boil, stirring continuously.

Cover the pan and simmer for 10 minutes. Melt the additional butter in a separate small saucepan. Add the apple to the butter, sprinkle with the sugar. Stir until the apple is coated with butter. Place a lid on the pan and cook gently until soft. Remove the lid, add the curry powder and fry for a minute. Add this apple and curry to the soup.

Add cream and spring onions, heat for a minute and add salt and pepper to taste.

Note: Because there are few ingredients in this soup you must use a well-flavoured chicken stock or it will be tasteless.

TOMATO AND CUCUMBER SOUP WITH AVOCADO GARNISH

INGREDIENTS

60 g (2 oz) butter

1 medium-sized white onion, finely diced

1 tablespoon flour

500 g (1 lb) ripe tomatoes

2 medium-sized green cucumbers

2 cups (16 fl oz) chicken stock

salt and pepper

½ cup (4 fl oz) cream

GARNISH

1 medium-sized avocado

This soup not only tastes good but looks very pretty with the garnish of diced green avocado. The soup can be made well beforehand and then reheated. However, because it discolours rapidly, the avocado must be diced only at the last moment.

Craig Claiborne is the food editor for the *New York Times* and while I was in America I came across this particular recipe which had appeared in his column. I found it interesting because we do not really think of using avocado in Australia as a garnish and yet it is most enjoyable to eat, as it is rich and bland in contrast to the slightly acidic taste of tomato.

Melt the butter in a saucepan and add the onion. Sauté, stirring occasionally until softened but do not let it brown. Add the flour and cook, stirring for a couple of minutes to fry the flour.

Dice the tomatoes into sections and squeeze out some of the seeds. See note on peeling at end of recipe if you use a blender. Add the tomato to the pan. Peel the cucumber and cut in halves lengthwise. Using a teaspoon, scrape out the seeds and slice the cucumber.

Add the cucumber to the pan with the stock and bring to the boil, stirring. Cover the pan and simmer gently for about 25 minutes or until the vegetables are quite soft.

Either put in a blender, or else moulin or sieve the mixture. If you do use a blender it may be wise to skin the tomatoes when you are preparing them.

Season to taste with salt and pepper. Leave to cool.

When serving reheat and add the cream. Sometimes the soup needs additional salt when you add cream.

Garnish

Cut the avocado into halves. Separate the two sections. Cut this into quarters and then peel the skin back. Cut into slices and then across into dice.

Scatter this over the top of the soup. It will warm through in about 1 minute and really does not need cooking.

Note: This soup keeps for several days, but do not add the cream or avocado until reheating.

WHITE VEAL STOCK

This stock can be used as a base for soups or in sauces when a light flavoured stock is needed. It is a little more trouble than the simple chicken stock but it keeps well and forms a lovely golden jelly. You need to boil it up about every 5 days if you don't use it all, or it can be frozen.

Place the veal bones and stewing veal with the salt in a very large saucepan. Add the water and bring very slowly to the boil. As it heats some scum will rise to the top; remove this with a spoon. The slower you bring the liquid to the boil, the clearer the stock will become.

When it comes to the boil, partially cover the pot leaving a little opening for the steam to escape and simmer for about an hour. Add the carrots, onion and leek and the bouquet garni and continue simmering for another 5 hours. The water should move gently without bubbling except for the odd bubble which will occasionally break the surface. The meat and bones should remain well covered by liquid at all times; if they are not, add a little extra water.

Turn the heat off, leave the pot to stand for about 20 minutes to settle. Trying not to stir it up too much, use a cup to remove the liquid from the pot, pour it through a strainer into a wide basin. This will give you a really clear stock. Leave to cool and then refrigerate.

Notes: This will not be salted sufficiently but it is much better to undersalt and then adjust the seasoning according to the dishes it is used in.

The vegetables are tasteless and useless. The meat will also be relatively tasteless but it could be minced and mixed with some herbs and mashed potatoes and then made into little patties.

When making this stock if you have any uncooked chicken bones, wings or necks they can also go into the pan with the veal. Don't use bones which have already been cooked as this will make the stock cloudy.

INGREDIENTS

1 kg (2 lb) veal bones, roughly chopped into big pieces
1 kg (2 lb) cheap stewing veal, diced into pieces
1 teaspoon salt
10 cups (3¾ pints) water
3 medium-sized carrots, diced or sliced
1 medium-sized onion, roughly diced
1 leek, cut into a few large pieces
A bouquet garni of 1 stalk celery, 3 sprigs parsley, 1 bay leaf and 1 sprig thyme

There is a variety of first courses, some cold, others hot, some light and the remainder a little more substantial.

If you use a very light first course choose a rich or heavier dish to follow. A more substantial first course should be followed by some nicely roasted chicken with a golden skin, a piece of baby lamb or a plainly cooked meat.

Whichever type of first course you choose, try to make it look as attractive as possible and your guests will happily anticipate the dish to follow.

HAM LOAF

INGREDIENTS
500 g (1 lb) ham
2 tablespoons vegetable oil
3 tablespoons water
2 tablespoons flour
3 teaspoons gelatine
1 tablespoon tomato paste
½ cup (4 fl oz) milk
pinch cayenne pepper
¾ cup (6 fl oz) cream

This loaf can be served as a first course in the same way you would normally serve a terrine or paté. It has a ham flavour but is lighter to eat than plain ham slices. It keeps really well and is improved by making at least the day before.

Mince the ham really finely or put it in a food processor. (If it isn't fine the texture is not so pleasant.) Place the oil and water in a small saucepan and bring to the boil. Mix the flour, dry gelatine and tomato paste together. This will be rather dry. Then stir in the oil and water and return to the pan. Mix until it is a smooth paste.

Add the milk and bring to the boil stirring continuously. It will be a thick and pasty mixture. Add the cayenne. Mix this into the ham, blending well with a fork. Add the cream, stir well to blend through.

This can be put in a log tin or a mould; to make it easy to turn out you can line the base of the tin with some foil or lightly oiled paper. Use one which holds about 4 cups (1½ pints). Press down firmly so there are no air bubbles. Chill until firm and then cut into thick slices.

FISH CREAM

INGREDIENTS
5 fillets of whiting, weighing about 60 g (2 oz) each
½ cup (4 fl oz) water
½ cup (4 fl oz) white wine
½ teaspoon salt

MIXTURE FOR THE CREAM
2 slices white bread, crusts removed
3 tablespoons water
1 clove garlic, crushed
2 tablespoons lemon juice
white pepper
salt
2 tablespoons mayonnaise

In this, one of the prettiest of all dishes, the fish is garnished with layers of egg, parsley and caviar in stripes. The dish can be served either in little individual servings as a first course or on a large platter with toast fingers as a savoury with drinks.

I have always made Fish Cream with fillets of whiting and found this the most successful. Other fish (fresh only) could be used but they need to be fine in texture as in this dish the fish is only lightly flaked and a coarse fish would form into more definite pieces which would give a different result.

After it has been chilled for a couple of hours, the natural glutinous quality of the fish forms the mixture into a mould.

Check that there are no small fin pieces left on the whiting. Feel down the fillets; although the fish man will have removed most of the bones, he usually leaves a tiny section at one end: cut a small V and remove these. This is the easiest and quickest way to remove these little bones from whiting and if handled carefully the fish will not break up.

Place the water, wine and salt in a frying pan. Bring to the boil. Add the whiting, bring the water down to a simmer. Turn fish after about 1 minute and cook on the other side.

Using a spatula or two forks, remove fish. Turn over and with a knife lightly scrape away the black skin. Using a fork, flake the fish into small pieces.

Mixture for the Cream

Place the bread in a basin. Cover with the water and let stand for several minutes. Press the water out of the bread, using your hands. Beat the bread with a fork to break it up. Add the garlic, lemon, white pepper, salt and mayonnaise and then mix in the flaked fish. Check seasoning.

Place in a bowl or on a plate and cover well. Refrigerate. This keeps for 24 hours.

Garnish

Cut the egg into halves. Remove the yolk. Cut the whites into very small dice. Push the yolk through a sieve.

Use a spatula to keep a straight line and sprinkle first some parsley in a strip on the fish, then the sieved yolk, then egg white and next the pink caviar. Continue until the surface is covered with the strips. Keep refrigerated.

Once you add the garnish Fish Cream should be refrigerated for only an hour or so as the egg becomes a little dry looking if left too long.

Notes: The fish sets firmly but when you want to serve, it can be broken up with a spoon or fork and spread out on a small platter. Only have this in a thin layer for the best effect.

Black caviar looks good but it imparts a rather nasty grey colour to the fish very quickly so I generally use the pink.

GARNISH
1 hard boiled egg
2 tablespoons parsley, finely chopped
1 x 45 g (1½ oz) jar pink caviar

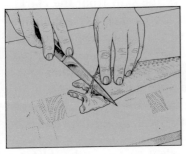

1. Whiting fillets as they are usually sold with the small fins on top. These are removed by cutting with a small sharp knife.

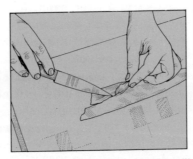

2. Cut a tiny V shaped section, this will enable you to remove the small bones from the top which always remain even in filleted whiting.

TERRINES

Terrines are so named because of the dish in which the mixture traditionally is cooked. They are not at all difficult to make and are a delight to eat. In general, they are best when made at least 24 hours before serving, during which time the flavour improves quite dramatically.

It is sensible to taste the mixture before baking. You can't taste it raw, so take a tiny spoonful out and cook it in a pan with a little butter. When cooked leave to cool and taste; you can then adjust the salt and pepper as you wish, remembering that as terrines are served cold they must be well seasoned.

To protect the sides and top of the terrine, line the dish with thin slices of bacon. This will keep it moist. You can stretch the bacon out using the back of a knife. Leave all the fat on as this is needed to keep the terrine from drying.

Terrines should always be baked Bain Marie (in a dish with water). When cooked, the mixture will shrink away from the sides and the liquid surrounding it will be quite transparent and free from pink or red juices. You can pierce it through the middle and the juices which bubble out should be clear also.

After the terrine is cooked, remove from the water and leave to cool for a short time then weight with a full tin of some type or a brick wrapped in foil if you are using a log shaped tin. This weight should stay on top for about 8 hours or until the mixture becomes firm enough to be easily sliced.

GREEN PEPPERCORN TERRINE

This is rather a firm terrine which slices very easily and keeps for about a week. The green peppercorns are spicy and the amount you use can be adjusted according to taste. If you have a mincer you can mince the meat yourself but often it is easier to have the entire amount ordered and minced by the butcher. It should be minced rather finely for easier slicing.

The bacon, veal and pork are minced finely and then mixed together in a large basin. Remove the skin from the chicken breasts. Cut into small dice. Cut the chicken livers into small pieces. Mix these with the minced meat, then add the peppercorns, eggs and salt.

You need to mix the terrine with your hands rather than a spoon. You should use one hand with the fingers open, as if it was a large fork and this mixing makes the terrine smooth.

Spread a loaf tin or terrine with bacon on the base and sides. Fill with the meat mixture then top with more bacon. Place in a moderate oven 180-190° C (350-375° F) in a dish which has water to come halfway up the outside of the dish.

Cook for approximately 1¼ hours or until the terrine has shrunk away from the sides a little. Remove from the oven, take out of the water and leave to stand, then place a weight, such as a tin, on top. Leave to stand until completely cold (about 4 hours), then refrigerate.

INGREDIENTS

250 g (8 oz) bacon
250 g (8 oz) veal
250 g (8 oz) lean pork
3 medium-sized chicken breasts, boned
250 g (8 oz) chicken livers
¼ cup (2 oz) green peppercorns, completely drained
2 eggs, beaten
1½ teaspoons salt

TO FINISH TERRINE
250 g (8 oz) bacon

EGGS STUFFED WITH PURÉE OF PEAS

Cut the hard boiled eggs into halves lengthwise and remove the yolks. Set aside.

Melt the butter in a saucepan and add the onion and lettuce. Sauté until slightly softened, stirring occasionally. Shell peas and add to saucepan with water, sugar and salt. Cover and cook until the peas are tender.

Drain well. Push the peas through a sieve or moulin. Push the yolks through the same sieve or moulin and mix with the pea purée. Add mayonnaise and, if needed, enough cream to make a moist mixture. Season with a little cayenne pepper.

Place the pea purée in a piping bag with a large star tube, something like a No. 7. Pipe the purée into each egg white, mounding it well.

Garnish

Peel the tomato, cut into quarters and then remove all the seeds leaving just the outside layer. Cut this into long strips. Decorate the top of each stuffed egg with a strip of tomato.

Serve these on a bed of watercress or with some Cucumber and Lychee Salad (see p. 118).

Note: Large eggs are served as a first course but if you wish, tiny eggs can be prepared and served as an appetiser with drinks.

Sufficient for 12 egg halves

INGREDIENTS
6 hard boiled eggs
30 g (1 oz) butter
1 small white onion, finely diced
2 leaves lettuce, finely diced
250 g (8 oz) fresh peas, or a 60 g (2 oz) packet dried peas
2 cups (16 fl oz) water
1 teaspoon sugar
½ teaspoon salt
1 tablespoon mayonnaise
a little cream (optional)
pinch cayenne pepper

TOMATO GARNISH
1 ripe tomato

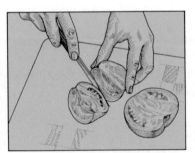

1. Using a sharp kitchen knife, cut a peeled tomato into quarters.

2. Remove the inside seeds, leaving just the outside section.

3. Cut this carefully into long strips to use as a garnish.

MOULDED SEAFOOD

This dish which is served cold is usually made with cooked prawns but crayfish can be used. This recipe has just enough gelatine to give the dish a good shape but it is served with a spoon and not sliced as it breaks when you begin serving it. Only a small quantity of seafood is specified; use more if you like.

Cook the unpeeled potatoes in a pot of salted water. Drain, leave to cool a little and skin them. Cut into neat cubes.

Mix the potatoes with the eggs, prawns, onion, pickling cucumber, parsley and season with a little salt and pepper.

Sauce

Mix the Oil Mayonnaise with the tomato sauce, Worcestershire sauce and horseradish relish.

In a small bowl mix the gelatine with the cold water, stir and then dissolve by standing in a pan of hot water. Add a little of the mayonnaise mixture to the warm gelatine and then add gelatine mixture to the mayonnaise. Stir this immediately into the prawn and potatoes.

Place the mixture into a mould or basin. Press down well using the back of a spoon to get rid of any air bubbles. Put in the refrigerator to set.

It can be eaten in about 4 hours.

Notes: This keeps for about 24 hours, but not much longer. Prawns do not usually keep for very long.

You can set the mixture in small individual dishes rather than a large mould if you prefer.

Wafer thin slices of fresh pineapple are an interesting accompaniment to Moulded Seafood.

INGREDIENTS
500 g (1 lb) potatoes, preferably new ones, unpeeled
salt
3 hard boiled eggs, roughly diced
500 g (1 lb) prawns, shelled and cut into small pieces
1 white onion, finely diced
¼ cup (1 oz) pickled cucumbers, diced small
1 tablespoon parsley, finely chopped
salt and pepper

SAUCE
1 cup (8 fl oz) well flavoured Oil Mayonnaise (see p. 42)
2 tablespoons tomato sauce
1 tablespoon Worcestershire sauce
2 teaspoons horseradish relish
3 teaspoons gelatine
3 tablespoons cold water

MUSHROOMS MONACO

For this dish you need mushrooms which form a cap when you remove the stalk. If you use flat ones, the filling will drip over. The mixture will fill 12 large mushrooms about 6 cm (2½ ins) in size. It is a little difficult to give an exact number of mushrooms as mushrooms vary from very deep to just medium caps.

Remove the stalks from the mushrooms. Season each cap with a little salt and pepper.

Remove the coral from the scallops. Place each scallop down and cut into thin slices. Place them overlapping on the mushrooms and scatter the pieces of coral over the top.

Garlic Butter

Mash the butter with garlic, parsley, lemon, salt and pepper. Dot tiny pieces of this over the scallops.

Garnish

Place the almonds in a dry frying pan and cook for a couple of

INGREDIENTS
12 to 18 mushrooms
a little salt and pepper
250 g (8 oz) scallops

GARLIC BUTTER
60 g (2 oz) butter
1 clove garlic, crushed
1 tablespoon parsley, finely chopped
1 teaspoon lemon juice
¼ teaspoon salt
white pepper

GARNISH
¼ cup (1 oz) blanched almonds, finely chopped

minutes, stirring until they are a light golden colour. Sprinkle on top of the scallops. Place on a well-buttered tray and bake in a moderate oven for about 10 to 12 minutes. Do not overcook or the scallops will toughen.

Notes: These can be prepared well beforehand and kept refrigerated. Cover them with foil or the butter tends to smell rather strong in the refrigerator.

The mushrooms can be served on little circles of buttered toast or else on circles of bread lightly fried in butter.

COUNTRY STYLE TERRINE

This terrine is very light and has a green colour from the spinach which is interspersed with studdings of ham, tongue and chicken livers. It needs gelatine to make it firm enough to cut easily and is better if made 24 hours before eating.

Place the minced pork into a large basin. Put the spinach in a saucepan and cook, without a lid, stirring occasionally so it will cook rather dry. It must not have any liquid in it. Add this spinach to the pork. Mix in the ham, tongue, eggs, onion, garlic, parsley, salt with the rosemary, basil, nutmeg and white pepper.

Using your hands mix everything together well. Use your hand rather like a spoon, with your fingers slightly open.

Mix the gelatine with the water in a cup and stir. Place this into a small saucepan and have water to come halfway up the outside of the cup. Heat, stirring until the gelatine is dissolved. Add the gelatine to the meat mixture and mix through.

Melt the butter in a small frying pan. Cut the livers into halves and remove any dark parts. Add to the butter and sauté for a moment until they have changed colour on the outside and stiffened slightly. Remove.

While the pan is hot add the cream and mix to get up any nice brown specks from the base of the pan. Cut the livers into small pieces and add with the cream to the mixture. Mix well.

Line a terrine dish or a square log tin with bacon. Fill with the meats and then top with more bacon. Cover the top with some foil and then a lid. If you use a loaf tin which does not have a lid, just tuck an extra thickness of foil well under the edges. Place in a baking dish with water to come halfway up the sides of the terrine and cook in a moderate oven 180-190° C (350-375° F) for about 1¼ hours or until it has shrunk away from the sides slightly. Remove the terrine. Cool for about 30 minutes and then place a weight, such as a tin, on top. Leave to stand for about 6 hours and then refrigerate.

Notes: You can buy tongue in small tins which can be used in this dish, making the preparation easier. There is usually some jelly around the tongue and this can also be added. Skin is usually to be found on tinned tongue; you can remove this.

INGREDIENTS
375 g (12 oz) pork fillet, finely minced
1 packet, about 250 g (8 oz) frozen spinach
125 g (4 oz) ham, diced small
125 g (4 oz) tongue, diced small
2 eggs
1 medium-sized white onion, finely diced
1 clove crushed garlic
1 tablespoon parsley, finely chopped
1 bare teaspoon salt
pinch rosemary
pinch basil
¼ teaspoon nutmeg
white pepper
1 tablespoon gelatine
¼ cup (2 oz) water
30 g (1 oz) butter
4 chicken livers
¼ cup (2 oz) cream

TO LINE TERRINE
250 g (8 oz) bacon

EGG AND ZUCCHINI MOULDS

Makes 6 large or 8 small moulds

INGREDIENTS
ZUCCHINI MIXTURE
375 g (12 oz) zucchini
½ teaspoon salt
45 g (1½ oz) butter
1 medium-sized white onion, finely diced
white pepper

EGG MIXTURE
45 g (1½ oz) butter
6 large eggs
¼ cup (2 oz) milk
salt

FRESH TOMATO SAUCE
500 g (1 lb) tomatoes
60 g (2 oz) butter
salt and pepper
½ teaspoon sugar

Zucchini Mixture

Wash, but do not peel zucchini, discard the ends. Grate and place in a bowl with the salt. Stir to mix the salt through the vegetable. Leave for about 1 hour. At the end of this time there will be quite a lot of moisture in the bowl. Squeeze the zucchini firmly between the palms of your hands and place on paper towelling to dry.

Melt the butter in a frying pan, cook the onion until just softened but not brown. Add the zucchini and stir with a fork until it is just softened. This only takes about 4 or 5 minutes. Season with a little pepper and leave to cool.

Egg Mixture

Melt the butter in a frying pan. Beat 4 of the eggs with milk and salt and add to the butter. Cook, stirring with a fork as if you were making scrambled eggs and remove while they are still creamy. Beat the remaining two eggs and mix into the cooked egg. Add the zucchini.

Tomato Sauce

Peel the tomatoes and then cut into quarters. Gently press the quarters together to squeeze out some of the seeds. Dice the tomatoes into small pieces.

Melt the butter and add the tomatoes. Cook, seasoning with salt, pepper and sugar, giving them an occasional stir for about 20 minutes until a thick sauce has formed. This is not sieved but served with little tomato pieces in it.

It can be prepared beforehand and then reheated.

To Cook Moulds

Butter some little soufflé dishes, ramekins, or you can use dariole moulds. So they will turn out easily, put a little circle of foil on the base.

Place some of the egg and zucchini mixture into the moulds. They can be kept aside ready for baking. Place them in a dish with water to come about halfway up the sides. Place a piece of foil lightly on top so the top will not toughen. Bake them in a moderate oven, 180-190° C (350-375° F) until they are just set. The timing varies on the moulds but they generally take about 25 minutes. Do not let them overcook although they must be just firm in the centre to touch. Turn out by running a knife around the edge.

Serve with a fresh tomato sauce.

Notes: This type of egg dish can be made with various other vegetables or even fish. You can substitute mushrooms or cooked spinach for the zucchini. Tiny pieces of diced lobster or prawns are also very good.

Moulded Seafood (page 34)

SPINACH AND EGG GRATIN

This is a simple dish which is made up of really fresh spinach lightly sautéed in butter and a lovely delicate onion sauce for the final baking. Do not make it with frozen spinach; it is too soft and puréed and has no texture.

Wash the spinach really well and remove any large stalks. Stack leaves together and cut into strips. Melt the butter in a large frying pan or a saucepan. Add the spinach and cook, stirring until it is softened and the butter is absorbed. This does not take long but unless you stir the underneath, the top remains too firm. It will only take about 4-5 minutes altogether to cook spinach through. Season with the salt, pepper and nutmeg.

Remove from stove and leave to cool.
Slice the eggs and place aside.

Sauce

Melt the butter in a saucepan and add the onions. Cook for a few minutes, stirring occasionally until slightly softened. Place a lid on the pan and cook or 'sweat' the onions until they are quite soft. Add the flour and fry, stirring for a few minutes until it is granulated but do not brown it. Add the milk, cook until the mixture is thickened and boiling, stirring constantly. It will not be very thick at this stage. Turn down the heat and leave to cook for about 5 minutes and it will thicken just slightly. This sauce should not be too thick, just enough to coat a spoon.

Season with salt and pepper and add cream, which will thin it again. Put this through a moulin, or sieve or in a blender so you have a smooth sauce.

To Assemble the Dish

You can prepare this in either 6 to 8 small ramekins or individual ovenproof dishes, or make one larger shallow casserole and serve from this. It is nicer to have shallow rather than deep dishes so you get maximum flavour from the sauce.

Butter the dish. Spoon just enough sauce over the base to coat it. Then spread the spinach out in one even layer. Top with the sliced egg. Cover the top with a generous layer of sauce. (You may have more sauce than you need but the remainder can be kept refrigerated and used with lamb, or over vegetables.) Top with some grated parmesan or tasty cheese. Cover and refrigerate for 24 hours.

To Cook

Bake in moderate oven 180-190° C (350-375° F) for about 20 to 25 minutes or until the top is bubbling.

Note: This makes a lovely luncheon dish and can be served with a platter of ham.

INGREDIENTS
1 bunch spinach
60 g (2 oz) butter
a little salt and pepper
a good pinch nutmeg
4 hard boiled eggs

SAUCE
60 g (2 oz) butter
4 medium-sized white onions, diced or
*   thinly sliced*
2 tablespoons flour
2 cups (16 fl oz) milk
salt and pepper to taste
½ cup (4 fl oz) cream

TOPPING
parmesan or tasty cheese, finely grated

Bacon and Lettuce Quiche (page 50)

PEA ROULADE

A roulade is really a flat soufflé which is baked in a Swiss Roll tin and then rolled over and filled with all sorts of delicious things. When you cut a roulade you have alternating layers of the light soufflé and filling; it looks pretty and makes a very light but interesting course.

INGREDIENTS

PEAS

500 g (1 lb) fresh peas
30 g (1 oz) butter
1 medium-sized white onion, finely diced
3 lettuce leaves, finely shredded
a couple of sprigs of parsley
1 cup water
1 teaspoon salt
1 teaspoon sugar

SOUFFLÉ MIXTURE

60 g (2 oz) butter
3 tablespoons flour
1 cup (8 fl oz) milk
1 cup (8 fl oz) pea purée
3 egg yolks
4 egg whites
salt and pepper as needed

FILLING

4 rashers, 185 g (5 oz) bacon
½ cup (4 oz) thick sour cream
a little white pepper
salt if needed, depending on saltiness of
*   bacon*
2 teaspoons mayonnaise

Preparation of the Tin

Butter a Swiss Roll tin and line with paper. Butter this really well; it is easiest if you melt some butter to do this. Sprinkle the paper with a layer of breadcrumbs made from stale bread and tip away any excess crumbs which do not stick.

Pea Purée

Shell the peas. Melt the butter in a saucepan and add the onion, lettuce leaves and parsley. Cook, stirring occasionally until the onion has slightly softened. Add the water, salt and sugar. Cover and cook until tender.

Drain, but keep the liquid, as sometimes you need to add a little. Push the peas through a sieve or moulin or blend them. If very thick and solid you can add a tablespoon or so of the liquid. The mixture must measure 1 cup.

Roulade

Melt the butter in a saucepan and add the flour. Cook for a few minutes until the flour is granulated in appearance but do not let it brown. Add the milk and cook, stirring until it comes to the boil. It will be very thick. Add the pea purée and cook gently for a couple of minutes.

Remove from the heat to cool a little. Add 3 egg yolks, one at a time. Season with a little salt and pepper.

Beat the egg whites until they hold stiff peaks. Do not over-beat, once they hold a peak on the end of a whisk this is sufficient. Fold about a third of the egg whites into the purée. It is often easiest to then gently tip this pea mixture down the sides of the remaining egg whites and fold the remainder in. Do not overfold, it doesn't matter if there are one or two little bits of egg white through.

Pour gently into the tin. Bake in a moderate oven 180-190° C (350-375° F) for about 15 to 18 minutes or until firm on top. The timing for a roulade is important, if overcooked it will crack as you roll it. To turn out, place a piece of buttered foil down on a bench. Tip the roulade onto this. You can then use the foil as support to fold the roulade over.

Spread the roulade with the filling. Using the foil gently turn it over, rolling lengthwise. You can place this back in the oven for 5 or 10 minutes to keep it warm.

Obviously a roulade which is prepared at the last moment is ideal for dinner. However it can be cooked during the day and then reheated. If you do this, completely finish the dish but to stop the roulade drying brush the outside of the roll with melted butter. Place on a heatproof platter and leave aside. Do not refrigerate. To heat, place the roll in a moderate oven and cover with foil placed loosely over the top. Heat for about 20 minutes.

Filling
Cut the bacon into dice or thin strips. Place them in a dry frying pan and cook, stirring occasionally until the fat is transparent and the bacon is crisp. Remove and drain on kitchen paper.

Mix with the sour cream, pepper, mayonnaise and salt if necessary. This doesn't need to be warm as the warmth of the roulade will heat the filling through sufficiently and this is not the type of dish which must be eaten really hot.

Notes: Do not be tempted to make this with frozen or dried peas because we did not find either of these particularly successful. The frozen peas had a lack of flavour and a watery taste and the dried ones made a firm, dry-textured roll. So it is really worth shelling fresh peas to prepare this dish.

Roulades, even if carefully cooked, occasionally crack when you roll them over. This may detract a little from the appearance but don't worry as the flavour will still be as good.

BEAN SHOOT AND CHICKEN SALAD

This can be served either as a light luncheon dish or as a first course in small lettuce cups or orange shells. It will only serve four as a luncheon dish but eight as an entrée.

Heat the oil in a large frying pan and add the onions. Sauté gently, stirring occasionally until the onions have softened. Do not let them go brown. Remove to a bowl. Set pan with oil aside.

Place each chicken breast between two pieces of wax paper and with a meat mallet or rolling pin flatten to the same thickness all over. Cut in halves lengthwise. Cut across in thin strips.

Add the strips of chicken to the same pan the onion was cooked in. There will probably be sufficient oil, if not, add an extra couple of teaspoons. Keep the heat under the pan high and toss the chicken breasts, seasoning with a little salt and pepper until they have changed colour. Add the chicken to the onions.

Add the bean shoots to the pan, season with a little salt and cook quickly until they are barely cooked. Do not overcook as they will soften a little in the dressing. Remove bean sprouts and mix gently with onions and chicken.

Dressing
Mix the mayonnaise, cream, curry powder and crushed garlic together in a small bowl.

While the salad ingredients are still warm, mix these with the dressing. Taste for seasoning and leave aside at room temperature. You can make this salad about an hour before serving but don't refrigerate as this will spoil the flavour.

INGREDIENTS
2 tablespoons peanut oil (more may be needed)
2 medium-sized white onions, finely sliced
3 chicken breasts, boned (see p. 60)
salt and pepper
250 g (8 oz) bean shoots

DRESSING
1 tablespoon and 2 teaspoons mayonnaise
2 tablespoons cream
½ teaspoon curry powder
1 clove garlic, crushed

EGGS IN ANCHOVY SAUCE

INGREDIENTS
6 hard boiled eggs

OIL MAYONNAISE
2 egg yolks
1 teaspoon French mustard
½ teaspoon dry, English-style mustard
¾ cup (6 fl oz) peanut or olive oil
2 tablespoons white vinegar

ANCHOVY SAUCE
1 x 45 g (1½ oz) tin flat anchovy fillets
¾ cup (6 fl oz) Oil Mayonnaise
white pepper
1 teaspoon tomato paste

FILLING
2 teaspoons mayonnaise
30 g (1 oz) butter, slightly soft
salt and pepper (use salt sparingly)
small white onion, finely grated
1 tablespoon cream

Oil Mayonnaise
Place the egg yolks and mustards in a bowl and mix well. Gradually add the oil, drop by drop, stirring as you go. When about half the oil has been added, thin with 1 tablespoon of the vinegar. Then, a little more quickly add the remaining oil. Finish with the last of the vinegar.

This mixture will taste a little strange as it is unsalted but the anchovies in the sauce supply more than enough salt. Remember, however, if you are making Oil Mayonnaise for another dish add about ¼ teaspoon salt in the beginning when mixing the yolks and mustards together.

You can make this mayonnaise in a food processor, blender or mixing bowl. If using a bowl, make sure that it is perfectly dry before you start mixing as the slightest trace of moisture makes the mixture curdle.

Oil Mayonnaise will keep for some days if stored covered in a cool part of the kitchen or refrigerator.

Anchovy Sauce
Crush the anchovies with a fork and mix into mayonnaise with the pepper and tomato paste. Keep refrigerated.

Filling
Cut the eggs into halves lengthwise. Remove the yolks. Place in a bowl and mash with a fork. Add mayonnaise, butter, very little salt, pepper, grated onion and cream. The mixture should be very moist. Fill the egg whites with mixture.

To Serve
Place the eggs filling side down. Make sure the tops of the eggs are dry. Coat eggs with a little Anchovy Sauce.

Usually two halves are sufficient as a first course.

Notes: This dish goes well with a little tomato salad and some buttered bread.

If you find the eggs a little salty cut the salt down in the anchovies. Place them on a plate and pour a little milk over the top. Leave to stand for about 10 minutes and then drain.

BAKED AVOCADO WITH WHITE WINE SAUCE

INGREDIENTS
4 hard boiled eggs
salt and pepper
30 g (1 oz) butter
250 g (8 oz) mushrooms, thinly sliced
2 large avocados or three smaller ones

The idea for this recipe came after a trip to America where, particularly in California, they have very imaginative ways of serving and cooking this fruit. Even though the avocado is cooked you must still choose ripe avocados. Because they discolour, they need to be sliced at the last moment but the remainder of the dish can be prepared beforehand. Only a small serving should be presented as it is extremely rich. This also makes an interesting luncheon dish.

Cut the hard boiled eggs into thin slices. Place in buttered ovenproof dish. Season. Melt the butter in a frying pan and add the mushrooms. Cook over high heat until the mushrooms are just tender. This should only take about a minute. Place into the dish on top of the egg.

When you are ready to put the dish in the oven cut the avocados into halves and remove the seeds. Peel the halves (usually if they are ripe the skin comes away easily). Place the halves down flat on a board and cut into thin slices.

Arrange, overlapping slightly, on top of the dish.

Sauce

This can be made beforehand and then reheated, but keep covered so a skin will not form on the top.

Melt the butter in a frying pan and add the white onion. Sauté, stirring occasionally until soft. Add the curry and cook for a few minutes to bring out the flavour. Add flour and fry, stirring until the flour is granulated. Do not let the flour brown. Add the white wine and chicken stock and stir constantly until the sauce is bubbling and lightly thickened. It will be thin at first but must be cooked to bring out the flavour and it will thicken slightly. Add the cream and then check for seasoning. The sauce should just coat a spoon lightly. Pour over the avocado slices.

Topping

Sprinkle the crumbs over the avocado and sauce and dot the top with the pieces of butter. Bake in a moderate oven 180-190° C (350-375° F) until it is bubbling at the edges and heated through. The top will not brown but if you would like this golden, put the casserole under the griller for a few minutes.

Notes: If you can buy them, the small white button mushrooms are probably best from the visual point of view; the darker mushrooms taste as nice but leave brownish marks on the eggs. The eggs and mushrooms can be placed in the dish during the day and the sauce prepared. Then the avocado can be sliced at the last moment.

One of the most important things with avocado is not to overcook it. It should only be warmed through, otherwise some of the flavour is lost and it may become bitter.

SAUCE
45 g (1½ oz) butter
1 medium-sized white onion, finely diced
1 teaspoon curry powder
1 tablespoon flour
¾ cup (6 fl oz) dry white wine
½ cup (4 fl oz) chicken stock
¼ cup (2 oz) cream

TOPPING
breadcrumbs made from stale bread
30 g)1 oz) butter, cut in small dice

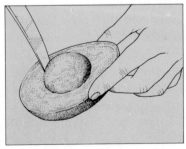

1. Cut avocado in halves and pull gently apart. Remove stone and skin.

2. Place flat side down and slice across with a sharp knife.

MUSHROOM MOULDS

You can either serve these mushrooms in the moulds or they can be turned out. The butter and crumb mixture which you use to coat the casserole gives a light outside crust and the inside is creamy in texture. Rather than the white button mushrooms which do not have so much flavour, use a darker mushroom.

INGREDIENTS

TO PREPARE CASSEROLES OR MOULDS
30 g (1 oz) butter
breadcrumbs made from stale bread

MUSHROOM MIXTURE
90 g (3 oz) butter
1 medium-sized white onion, finely diced
1 clove garlic, crushed
500 g (1 lb) mushrooms, thinly sliced
salt and pepper
1 cup (8 fl oz) dry white wine
4 large eggs
½ cup (4 fl oz) cream
2 tablespoons breadcrumbs made from stale bread
2 tablespoons parsley, finely chopped
pinch tarragon
pinch nutmeg
125 g (4 oz) ham, diced small

To Prepare Casseroles or Moulds

Melt the butter and brush the base and sides of the dish — you can use any shape; little soufflé dishes or oval ramekins. Spoon some crumbs in each dish and turn so the crumbs stick to the butter on the base and sides, then tip out any excess crumbs.

Mushroom Mixture

Melt the butter in a frying pan and sauté the onion and garlic until they have softened but do not let them brown. Add the mushrooms, turn up the heat and stir and cook. Season with salt and pepper and cook until the mushrooms have just barely softened. Then add the white wine to the pan and cook over high heat until it has evaporated completely.

Remove to a bowl and leave the mushrooms to cool slightly. Add to this the eggs, cream, breadcrumbs, parsley, tarragon, nutmeg and ham. Beat well with a fork. Pour this mixture into the prepared dishes.

To Cook

Place the little moulds in a baking tin with very hot water to come about halfway up the sides. Place a piece of foil loosely over the top of them. Bake in a moderate oven 180-190° C (350-375° F) until they are just set in the middle. Timing is rather difficult to give for this as it depends on the type of casserole or dish that you use. It can vary from 25 minutes up to 35 or 40 minutes.

When they are just set, remove from the oven and leave them to stand for about another 5 minutes.

To Turn Out

Run a knife around the edge of the casserole. Give them a gentle shake to loosen them from the base. Invert over a plate. Usually they are quite easy to handle. Serve immediately.

Note: This dish can be varied with other things. For example you can add some grated tasty cheese to the egg mixture, cook some bacon with the onion and garlic and then omit the ham. With salad it is a good lunch dish, although for lunch it would only really serve 4 people.

SAVOURY PASTRIES
PASTRY

These pastries are very good either for lunch or as a first course. I have included a couple of recipes for quiche plus some more unusual dishes. I always use a very thin layer of pastry in the dishes that I cook and try to handle it as quickly as possible to keep it light and crisp. There is a special note included on pastry and the easiest way to handle it.

Most people seem to be a little nervous about making pastry although it has become much simpler with the advent of the food processor. One of the main steps is to blend the flour and butter perfectly together so that the butter is in small pieces, each coated with flour. If you have warm hands (or during hot weather) the butter and flour can be blended by using two knives. The eggs and liquid are then added to the centre and the entire mixture blended together until it just forms a mass. Once blended stop immediately; you can then chill the dough or freeze it.

To Roll Pastry

When I first began demonstrating I had trouble with pastry because the strong overhead lighting in the demonstration kitchen made it soften very quickly. Flouring a bench is not good for pastry, it incorporates far too much flour into the mixture, altering the composition and so I worked out a method of rolling between wax paper which works really well even in hot weather. With buttered and sweet pastries this method is particularly good, as these types of pastries, very short in texture, break easily when handling them.

Place a large piece of wax paper on the bench, dust it lightly with flour and shake away the excess. Form the pastry into a circle and place on the paper. Then put another piece of waxed paper on top. Now roll across once with the rolling pin. Lift the top paper as it will now have stuck, put it back on top, turn over, lift the bottom one and replace and then roll again. It usually takes only a few rolls to make the pastry the correct size. Note that each time you roll the pin over the top you must move the paper and if it tears replace with another sheet of wax paper. Usually pastry rolled like this takes 2 minutes.

When you have the correct size lift away the top sheet. Leave the pastry on the bottom sheet of wax paper; lift with the paper and turn down into the flan tin or tart base. The paper will now be on top. Peel this away. If it is sticky you can put the entire thing, paper and pastry, into the refrigerator for about 5 minutes, then the paper can be removed easily. Press into the tin, moulding gently on the sides and cut away any excess on the edges.

It is best to have the sides a little thicker than the base so you can leave a little extra pastry on the side if you wish and press it over to give extra thickness. Bake as directed in the various recipes, most of which require baking blind.

Note: If the pastry wasn't chilled in the first place, you can now chill the case for 20-30 minutes before baking.

ASPARAGUS QUICHE

INGREDIENTS

1 pre-baked quiche case, 25 cm (10 in)
(see p. 50)

FILLING

500 g (1 lb) asparagus
30 g (1 oz) butter
2 tablespoons oil
3 medium-sized white onions, thinly sliced
salt and pepper
½ cup (4 fl oz) chicken stock
2 eggs
¾ cup (6 fl oz) cream
¼ cup (1 oz) gruyère cheese, grated
white pepper
¼ teaspoon salt

Break the asparagus at the point where it bends and then peel the stems using a vegetable peeler or small knife. This is terribly important, otherwise the stalks are far too tough in the quiche. It is best to buy fat stalks for this recipe as they are easier to peel than thin ones. Place the asparagus on a board and cut into diagonal pieces. Leave the tips in one large piece.

Melt the butter and oil in a frying pan and add the onions. Sauté, stirring occasionally until the onions are slightly softened. Add the pieces of asparagus and turn up the heat to high. Cook and stir until they are tipped with little golden bits but do not let them soften down. Add a little salt and pepper and the stock.

Keeping the heat high, boil this rapidly until the stock has formed a glaze over the asparagus. It will soften just a little as it cooks but don't let it become limp. This is another reason to buy the fat stalks as the little ones can break up.

Remove from the heat and place in a shallow basin to cool as quickly as possible so it will keep a bright green colour.

Beat the eggs, cream, gruyère cheese and mix with the onion and asparagus. Season.

Pour into the pre-baked shell and bake in moderate oven at 180-190° C (350-375° F) until the centre is just set. This usually takes about 25 minutes.

Leave to cool for 5 minutes before serving.

MUSHROOM AND CHAMPAGNE GALETTE

INGREDIENTS

TO ASSEMBLE

500 g (1 lb) puff pastry
1 egg to glaze
pinch salt

FILLING

60 g (2 oz) butter
2 large white onions thinly sliced
another 30 g (1 oz) butter
250 g (8 oz) mushrooms, cut into thin
  slices
salt and pepper
1 cup (8 fl oz) dry champagne
1 tablespoon flour
½ cup (4 fl oz) cream
1 egg

Galette literally means 'a big round cake'. This particular galette is a round pastry which is filled with a highly-flavoured mushroom mixture. It is a recipe which I made up for a party one night and have since used it over and over. It can be made and reheated although is really nicest if you prepare the dish and leave it refrigerated until you want to bake the galette.

Instead of champagne, a dry white wine could be used in the mushrooms, the quantity used is only small and the idea is that you can then drink the remainder of the bottle with the dish.

Filling

Melt the 60 g butter in a frying pan and cook the onions, stirring occasionally until they are quite soft. Remove from the pan.

Melt the remaining butter and add the mushrooms. Turn up the heat and cook, stirring until they are tender. This only takes about 1 minute. Season with salt and pepper. Return the onions to the same pan, add the champagne and boil rapidly until there is no liquid left and the onion and mushroom is glazed.

Mix the flour, cream and egg together, stirring until smooth. Add to the hot mushroom mixture and stir. It should thicken immediately and as soon as it does, remove from the heat and spread out on a dinner plate to become cool.

The filling must be quite cold before you use it.

Roll out the puff pastry thinly. Cut out two circles, each about 23 cm (9 in). Place one down on a buttered scone tray or oven tray. Spread the mushroom filling across to within 2.5 cm (1 in) of the edge. Place the other circle over the top. Pinch-pleat the edges together, checking that there are no gaps.

Beat the egg for glazing with the pinch of salt. Brush this around the edges of the pastry and over the top. You can decorate with some little crescents cut from the remaining scraps of pastry if you wish. Glaze these also. Cut a slit in the centre for the steam to come away and then keep refrigerated until you are ready to bake the galette. It can be kept for 12 hours at this stage.

To Cook
Bake in moderate oven, 190-200° C (375-400° F) for 20-25 minutes.

Notes: When buying mushrooms for this dish, choose ones that have darker brown undersides as these have more flavour. You can add a little diced ham, if you wish, to the mushrooms (about half a cup is sufficient) but the flavour of the mushrooms becomes so intensified by the champagne that they are sufficient on their own.

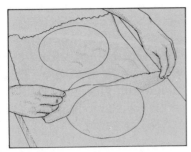

1. Roll out the puff pastry thinly and then cut out two circles approximately 23cm (9in) in diameter.

2. Spread the mushroom filling in an even layer on one of the circles, leaving a small strip of pastry free.

3. Place the second circle over the top of the filling and pinch the edges firmly together. Brush edges and top with the egg glaze and decorate with some cut-outs if you wish.

CRAYFISH QUICHE

INGREDIENTS
1 pre-baked quiche shell, about 23 cm
(9 in) or 25 cm (10 in)

FILLING
60 g (2 oz) butter
1 bunch spring onions, cut in chunky
pieces, with a little of the green topping
1 firmly packed cup (5 oz) crayfish, diced
small
1 tablespoon brandy
2 teaspoons tomato paste
2 teaspoons dry sherry
½ teaspoon salt
pinch cayenne pepper
2 eggs
¾ cup (6 fl oz) thick cream

Crayfish is an extravagance because it has become so expensive but in a quiche a small amount goes quite a long way. If you don't want to use crayfish, other seafoods could be substituted in the same quantity, for example, crab, chopped prawns or pink salmon are equally delicious.

This mixture is sufficient to fill a shallow quiche shell but not a deep one.

Melt the butter in a frying pan and add the spring onions. Cook for a moment only, until they become just limp. Add the crayfish and toss in the butter. Pour over the brandy, heat and light. Be careful when you do this as brandy can flare up. Remove the crayfish to a bowl.

In another small bowl place the tomato paste, dry sherry, salt, cayenne, eggs and cream and beat well with a fork. Sometimes the tomato paste stays in lumpy pieces, so make sure it is evenly mixed. Use only a fork when beating as a whisk gives bubbles and froth on top of the quiche.

To Assemble
Place the crayfish and spring onions on the base of the quiche case. Spread it out evenly. Pour the egg mixture over the top. Bake in a moderate oven 180-190° C (350-375° F) for about 25 minutes, or until it is just firm on top. Be careful not to overcook. Leave to stand for 5 minutes before serving.

Notes: The crayfish and egg can be prepared beforehand but only pour into the quiche shell when you are baking it. This quiche is nicest slightly warm although still quite good cold. It can be made and then reheated gently for about 10 minutes if you wish.

ZUCCHINI WRAPPED IN FILO

INGREDIENTS
6 zucchini, small to medium-size

STUFFING
60 g (2 oz) butter
1 large white onion, finely diced
250 g (8 oz) mushrooms, thinly sliced
salt and pepper
1 cup (8 fl oz) dry white wine
6 slices ham, cut fairly thin
filo pastry
butter

Bring a pot of salted water to the boil. Discard the ends from the zucchini. Add vegetables to the water and cook gently until just tender. Be careful not to overcook. Remove from the water and drain. Place in a colander and gently run cold water over them to cool the zucchini. When cool, cut them in halves lengthwise. Using a teaspoon remove the seeds from the centres and discard. When you cut them into halves be sure to keep the halves together otherwise you will have trouble pairing them up later.

Stuffing
Melt the butter in a frying pan and add the onion. Cook gently, stirring occasionally until softened. Add the mushrooms, season with salt and pepper, turn up the heat to high and cook rapidly until just softened. This usually takes only a minute. Add the white wine and boil until all the wine has completely gone. It will soak in and flavour the mushrooms. Leave this to cool a little and then fill the zucchini halves with the mushrooms.

Pair them together again, pressing gently to hold them firmly. Wrap in ham.

Filo

While you are handling filo pastry, the remaining sheets should be kept covered with a damp piece of kitchen paper or dampened tea towel to prevent them from drying. If some brands of filo have too much flour on the sheets, this can be brushed away using a dry pastry brush. However the different brands vary considerably, and this may not always be necessary.

Melt some butter in a small saucepan. The quantity is hard to give as it depends on the size of the zucchini. Place a strip of filo, just a little wider than the zucchini, down on the bench. Brush with melted butter. Place another sheet the same size on top and brush with butter. Put the zucchini on one end and roll over. You do not need too many layers of filo so you can trim a bit from the ends. Brush the outside lightly again with butter.

Place on a lightly greased baking sheet and then refrigerate until you want to bake these. Bake in moderately hot oven, 190-200° C (375-400° F) for about 20 to 25 minutes until the outside pastry is crisp and golden.

These can be prepared 4 to 5 hours before you cook them.

Notes: Occasionally some moisture comes out of the zucchini and the pastry doesn't go crisp in the centre. The taste will not be quite the same but it is still very good. If you would like a sauce with these, either a White Wine Sauce (see p. 42) such as the one used to top the avocado or else a light fresh Tomato Sauce (see p. 36) is good.

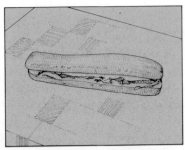

1. Fill the zucchini halves with mushroom filling and press together firmly.

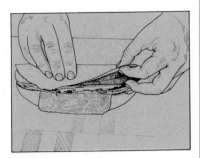

2. Wrap each of the zucchinis in a piece of thinly sliced ham.

3. Brush two layers of filo with melted butter and roll up each zucchini.

PASTRY FOR QUICHE

INGREDIENTS

SOUR CREAM PASTRY

1 cup (4 oz) flour
pinch salt
125 g (4 oz) butter, cut in small pieces
2 tablespoons thick sour cream
raw beans for baking

I have tried many pastries for the various quiches but still find this one the most successful. It is very light and flaky.

Sift the plain flour with the salt into a large basin and add the pieces of butter. Then either cut this into crumbly pieces with two knives or crumble with your fingers. Add the sour cream and mix gently until it holds together. Knead very lightly and roll out. If it is sticky it can be chilled for about 30 minutes.

Line a tin with the pastry. Cover the pastry with some greaseproof paper or foil, although foil often causes a certain amount of steaminess. If you use greaseproof, butter it lightly; I generally use a double thickness. You can prick the base of the pastry, but be careful that you do not leave any little holes for the filling to come through.

Fill the paper in the pastry case with some raw beans, such as kidney or haricot beans and bake in a moderate oven 180-190° C (350-375° F) until set, about 20 to 25 minutes. Carefully remove the paper and beans and return the pastry shell to the oven to dry out for a few minutes.

When you pre-bake a case for a quiche the pastry is much more successful. The baked case can be frozen or kept in an air-tight tin for a couple of days.

BACON AND LETTUCE QUICHE

INGREDIENTS

1 pre-baked pastry case, 25 cm (10 in)

BACON AND LETTUCE FILLING

2 medium-sized white onions
8 to 10 large lettuce leaves
60 g (2 oz) butter
salt and pepper
3 rashers, 125 g (4 oz), bacon
2 eggs
½ cup (4 fl oz) thick cream
¼ teaspoon salt

TOMATO TOPPING

2 ripe tomatoes
salt and pepper
1 teaspoon sugar
2 tablespoons gruyère cheese, grated
1 tablespoon parmesan cheese, finely grated

Bacon and Lettuce Filling

Cut the onions into halves and then into thin slices.

If lettuce has been washed, make sure that it is completely dry. Remove the tough white section from the base of the lettuce leaves and place them on top of each other. Shred rather finely. Do not use the very green outside leaves of the lettuce as they remain rather chewy in the quiche.

Melt the butter and add the onions, sauté, stirring for about 2 minutes. Add the lettuce, sprinkle with a little salt and pepper and cook, stirring occasionally until both are quite tender. The best way to judge is to taste the lettuce as timing varies according to the season.

Cut the rashers of bacon into small strips. Place in a separate frying pan and cook, stirring, until the fat is transparent and bacon slightly crisp. Drain on kitchen paper. When the lettuce and onion are tender, mix with the bacon in a bowl. Beat the eggs, cream and salt in a small basin and stir into the lettuce and bacon. Pour this into the quiche case.

Tomato Topping

Peel the tomatoes and cut into thin slices. Arrange these over the lettuce. Sprinkle with a little salt, pepper and sugar. Mix the two cheeses together. Sprinkle over the top of the tomato.

Bake in moderate oven 180-190° C (350-375° F) for about 35-40 minutes or until the top is golden and the egg filling is just set. Leave for about 5 minutes before cutting.

CHICKEN

Due to commercial production chicken has become one of the most reasonably priced high protein meats. It is always reliably tender and can be enhanced by flavourings either added to the meat or put in accompanying sauces.

One of the advantages of modern shopping is that you can purchase portions separately, such as breasts, or legs, and this makes it easy to prepare many dishes. When you buy a fresh chicken it should always have loose skin, firm flesh and there should never be any odour at all. When you bring home chicken in a plastic bag be sure to remove the bag and wash the chicken as the blood which collects will make the meat spoil. Pat the chicken dry and then keep loosely covered in the refrigerator.

TO PORTION A CHICKEN

If you portion a chicken this way you will have nine even-sized pieces which will all cook in the same amount of time.

1. Remove chicken leg, separate thigh and drumstick at the joint.

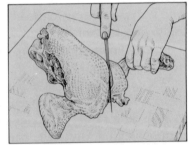

2. Cut through at the joint, including a small portion of the breast meat.

3. Hold the body upwards and cut down, removing the breast.

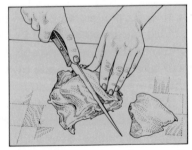

4. Cut the breast into three equally sized portions.

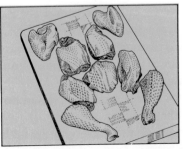

5. Leg and thigh portions, wing and breast portions.

BRAISED DUCK

INGREDIENTS

1 duck 2 kg (4 lb)
salt and pepper
1 sprig of thyme
large sprig of parsley
½ cup (4 fl oz) white wine
½ cup (4 fl oz) chicken stock

VEGETABLES

4 small turnips
8 small potatoes
8 small white onions
90 g (3 oz) butter
salt, pepper and a little sugar
1 tablespoon water (or white or red wine)
2 tablespoons parsley, finely chopped

The duck is cooked first in the oven and then for a few minutes more with vegetables. With this moist cooking it becomes wonderfully tender and full of flavour. This type of dish can be reheated most successfully. For general notes on the purchasing and preparation of duck, see page 63.

Remove the fat from the tail of the duck and salt and pepper the bird. Remove the lower wing part. Truss. Prick the skin around the thighs, back and lower breast using a sharp fork. Put the thyme and parsley inside the centre cavity.

Place the duck in a covered casserole in a moderately hot oven, 200° C (425° F) for about 15 minutes, breast side up. Prick the skin again. Then replace the lid on the casserole and continue cooking for another 30 minutes. Take the casserole from the oven and tip out all the fat. Add the white wine and stock and place a lid on the casserole. Continue cooking until the duck is tender, about 1¼ to 1½ hours.

Vegetables

Peel the turnips and cut them into halves or quarters. Place in cold water and bring to the boil. Cook 1 minute, drain and leave aside. Peel the potatoes and if large cut into halves or quarters. Trim the onions, leave a tiny bit of the root end on so they will not fall to pieces.

Place the potatoes in a pot of cold, salted water and bring them to the boil. Cook, covered about 5 minutes. Drain.

Melt 30 g (1 oz) of butter in a saucepan. Add the blanched turnips, season with salt, pepper and a little sugar and cook gently until glazed. Add 1 tablespoon water, cover the saucepan and cook until the turnips are tender. Leave aside.

Melt another 30 g (1 oz) butter and add the onions. Season with salt, pepper and sugar and toss until glazed and quite golden on the outside. Add 1 tablespoon water (or you can use white or red wine) and cook, covered until tender. The onions will take about 25 minutes to cook. Remove and leave aside with the turnips.

Melt the remaining 30 g (1 oz) butter and add the potatoes. Season with salt and pepper and cook, shaking occasionally until tender and quite crisp and golden on the outside. Add the potatoes to the other vegetables.

To Assemble the Dish

When the duck is cooked, remove from the oven and cut the trussing strings. Remove the fat from the top. There will be a little but not a lot of fat as most was discarded in the preliminary cooking. Tip the liquid into a saucepan and boil rapidly until reduced to about half. Check seasoning.

Add about 30 g (1 oz) of unsalted butter, cut in pieces and just let the butter melt in the heat of the sauce.

Place the vegetables on the base of the casserole. Sprinkle with parsley.

Remove the legs and then wings from the duck. Place the

duck on its back and then cut down along each side of the breast bone. Remove the entire breast from each side. Place on a board, cut the breast lengthwise in thin slices. Arrange the duck portions over the vegetables. Coat the duck with the sauce.

Place a lid on the casserole, return to the oven, and cook another 10 minutes for all the flavours to mingle.

Notes: This can be prepared completely to the stage of leaving in the casserole, with the duck carved. Then reheat a little longer so the vegetables and duck will be quite hot.

The sauce may be slightly thickened if you prefer, but it is really just like a lovely juice and shouldn't be made too heavy. Use a little cornflour, about 2 teaspoons would be plenty, if you wish to make a sauce which has more coating texture.

CHICKEN IN ASPARAGUS SAUCE

This dish has a light green sauce with a lovely flavour but for a good colour it is important to choose tinned asparagus that is bright green rather than the pale variety. Made in larger quantities, it is a very good party or buffet dish as it reheats through most successfully.

Cut the chicken into 9 portions. Melt the butter in a frying pan and sauté the chicken, turning, until it is golden on the outside. Season with a little salt and pepper as you do this.

Remove from the pan. Warm the brandy and light it; pour this over the chicken.

Sauce

Melt the butter in a saucepan and add the onions. Sauté, stirring occasionally until they are softened but not brown. Add the flour and cook for a few minutes, stirring. Add the champagne or white wine and stir until it comes to the boil. Place the chicken in a casserole. Pour the sauce over the top and place a lid on the casserole. Cook in a moderate oven 180-190° C (350°-375° F) for about 45 minutes or until the chicken portions are quite tender.

Drain the asparagus and push it through a sieve. When the chicken is tender, remove from the casserole and tip the sauce into a saucepan. Add the asparagus and cream, season with salt and pepper and then cook for a couple of minutes until blended. If too thin, boil rapidly until it has thickened a little.

Place the chicken portions in a shallow buttered casserole. Coat with the sauce.

Topping

Mix the breadcrumbs and cheeses together. Sprinkle this over the top of the chicken and sauce. Leave aside for reheating.

Cook in the oven until heated through and the top is golden and bubbling.

INGREDIENTS
1 chicken, 1.5 kg (3 lb)
30 g (1 oz) butter
salt and pepper
2 tablespoons brandy

SAUCE
45 g (1½ oz) butter
2 medium-sized white onions, finely diced
1 tablespoon flour
1 cup (8 fl oz) champagne or dry white wine
1 tin asparagus
⅓ cup (2½ fl oz) cream
salt and pepper as needed

TOPPING
3 tablespoons breadcrumbs made from stale bread
¼ cup parmesan cheese, finely grated
2 tablespoons gruyère cheese, grated

CHICKEN WITH LEMON SAUCE

INGREDIENTS

1 chicken, 1.5 kg (3 lb)
60 g (2 oz) butter
2 tablespoons brandy
1 clove garlic, crushed
rind of 1 lemon, grated
1 tablespoon flour
¼ cup (2 fl oz) lemon juice
1 cup (8 fl oz) chicken stock
1 teaspoon tomato paste
1 tablespoon sugar
1 tablespoon red currant jelly
¼ cup (2 fl oz) pure cream

LEMON SHREDS

1 lemon
saucepan water

Cut the chicken into 9 portions. Melt half the butter in a frying pan, add the chicken portions, a few at a time and cook, turning until golden on the outside. Heat the brandy separately. Remove the pan with the chicken from the heat, light the brandy and pour over the chicken. This is safer than adding brandy over heat when using butter; it can flare rather alarmingly.

Place the chicken pieces in a casserole so they fit just slightly overlapping. Pour over the juices and brandy.

Melt the remaining 30 g (1 oz) butter in the same pan. Add the garlic and lemon rind, then the flour and cook until the flour is slightly granulated but not brown. Add lemon juice, chicken stock, tomato paste, sugar and red currant jelly. Bring to the boil, stirring constantly until thickened, making sure that the red currant jelly is dissolved. Add the cream and heat.

Pour this sauce over the chicken pieces. Place into a moderate oven 180-190° C (350-375° F) and cook, uncovered for about 45 minutes, or until the chicken portions are tender. Baste several times while the chicken is cooking. While cooking, the sauce will thicken. Remove the chicken portions, coat with the sauce and sprinkle some lemon shreds over the top to serve.

Lemon Shreds

Using a vegetable peeler, remove thin strips from the lemon being very careful not to take any of the white part. Cut these into thin slivers the size of matches. Place them in the saucepan with water and bring to the boil. Simmer gently until quite tender; they won't take long as they are so thin. Drain.

To prevent them from drying, keep them in a small bowl of water and then drain on absorbent paper before using.

Notes: This chicken dish reheats successfully and can be made about 12 hours beforehand if you wish. Because of the slightly sweet and sour flavour it goes best with rice and salad but doesn't seem to be particularly good with vegetables.

Chicken Breasts with Ham and Spinach (page 59)

BABY CHICKENS IN TARRAGON SAUCE

You can buy baby chickens in some poultry shops or butchers, but generally they are not sold in supermarkets. If you cannot get baby chickens buy a larger chicken and cut into portions.

Cut the baby chickens into halves. Place each half down on a bench and press down to flatten slightly.

Heat the butter and oil in a frying pan and add the chickens. Unless your pan is very large you will need to do them in two batches or even three. Brown on both sides.

Remove the chicken halves and season well with salt and pepper. Wipe out the pan.

Sauce

Melt the butter and add the bacon. Cook until the bacon fat is transparent. Add the garlic and flour. Fry the flour for a few minutes until it is granulated. Do not brown it.

Cut the tomatoes into quarters, squeeze out some of the seeds, then dice the tomato. Add to the pan with tarragon, sugar, white wine, a little salt and pepper (not too much as the sauce will be reduced and it will become too salty). Cook until the sauce is reduced by about half.

Add the cream to the sauce and remove from the heat. Place the chickens in a large shallow ovenproof casserole. They can be placed slightly overlapping. If you do not have a large enough casserole, use two. Coat with the sauce.

Place into a moderate oven 180-190° C (350-375° F) and cook, basting with the sauce until the chickens are tender. Because they are so small, they won't take long, perhaps about 30-45 minutes.

The sauce should be of a good coating consistency. If it becomes thin in the oven you can easily rectify this. Place the sauce in a saucepan on the stove and boil rapidly and it will thicken in a few minutes.

The chickens are served with a little of the sauce to coat them.

Notes: Use a dry white wine but not one which has too much acid or it will be too sharp with the chicken.

Make sure that when you buy dried tarragon it has a good aroma. If it is kept too long in the shop it may smell musty. Russian tarragon is the usual variety grown in herb gardens in Australia and this doesn't have a great deal of flavour. If you can obtain some French tarragon this is much more aromatic.

INGREDIENTS

3 baby chickens, 500 to 750 g (1 lb to
1½ lb) each
30 g (1 oz) butter
1 tablespoon vegetable oil
salt and pepper

SAUCE

60 g (2 oz) butter
60 g (2 oz) bacon, diced small
1 clove garlic, crushed
2 teaspoons flour
1 large or two small ripe tomatoes, peeled
½ teaspoon dried tarragon, or about
2 teaspoons fresh tarragon, finely
chopped
pinch sugar
dry white wine
salt and pepper to taste
½ cup (4 fl oz) cream

Prawns Baked with Feta (page 98)

SPLIT CHICKEN WITH MUSHROOM STUFFING

INGREDIENTS
1 chicken, 1.5 kg (3 lb)
salt and pepper

TO COOK
30 g (1 oz) butter

STUFFING
30 g (1 oz) butter
1 white onion, finely diced
125 g (4 oz) mushrooms, diced small
salt and pepper
squeeze lemon juice
60 g (2 oz) butter
1 clove garlic, crushed
good pinch mixed herbs
2 chicken livers
1 cup (4 oz) breadcrumbs
1 egg

In this dish the chicken is stuffed under the skin so that the stuffing both flavours the flesh and keeps it moist. The skin crisps to a lovely golden brown and looks beautiful. Because of the way it is split one chicken will serve only four people so for six people do two chickens. The remainder is delicious cold.

Place the chicken on a board with its back towards you. Split the chicken the entire length of the back, cutting as close as possible to the backbone. Open it out with the skin side towards you. With your hand press down hard; you will hear a distinct crack as you do this. The chicken should be sitting fairly flat on the board. If not you will have to give it another firm thump with a rolling pin.

Cut away the wing tip at the second joint.

Put your fingers between the skin and the flesh. As you do this you will feel little membranes which are very easily broken with your fingers. Be careful not to tear the skin. Separate the skin, first from one breast and then the other. Then you can actually put your whole hand in and remove the skin from the leg section. If by any chance it does tear, patch with a needle and cotton because any holes will allow the stuffing to escape. Season the skin of the chicken with salt and pepper.

Stuffing

Melt the butter and add the onion. Cook, stirring occasionally until the onion has softened. Add the mushrooms, turn up the heat and cook, seasoning with salt, pepper and a squeeze of lemon until just softened. There shouldn't be any liquid in the pan. Remove the mixture and leave to cool.

Cream the 60 g (2 oz) butter until soft, add garlic and herbs. Mix in the cold cooked onion and mushroom. Cut the chicken livers into tiny pieces and add with the breadcrumbs and egg.

To Stuff the Chicken

Take a handful of the stuffing at a time and push it into place under the skin. You can almost work it down from the outside. Push it over the legs and drumsticks first and then do the breast last. Pat the skin back into place.

To Cook

Melt the butter. Brush the skin of the chicken with butter and leave aside for the butter to set on the skin. Place the chicken in a shallow ovenproof dish. Cook in a moderate oven 180-190° C (350-375° F) for about 50 minutes to 1 hour. Because it is flattened it will cook a little quicker than a chicken which is left in its original shape. The skin should be golden but if it is going too brown, cover with a piece of aluminium foil.

Remove from the oven. Cut into four portions to serve.

Note: You can use this idea with many stuffings. Keep the stuffing well flavoured and moist with butter.

CHICKEN BREASTS WITH HAM AND SPINACH

Place the chicken breasts between wax paper and flatten gently so they are an even thickness.

Wash the spinach well and remove any very tough stalks. Place the spinach down on a board and stack several layers together. Cut into shreds with a knife.

Sauce

It is advisable to make the sauce first as it usually takes longer to cook than the chicken.

Put the white wine, chicken stock and cream in a saucepan. Boil rapidly until the mixture has been reduced by about two-thirds. It will be slightly thickened. Leave aside.

Cut the unsalted butter into about 6 pieces. Leave aside. Melt the 60 g (2 oz) butter. When very hot add the chicken breasts and cook, turning once until tender. They only take a few minutes. Season with salt and pepper.

Remove the chicken breasts and wrap each one in a slice of ham. Put on a warmed platter and cover with foil. Place in the oven to keep warm.

Add the spinach shreds to the same pan you cooked the chicken in; there will be plenty of butter left. Cook rapidly until just limp; this only takes a couple of minutes. Season. Add the spinach to the sauce.

Remove from the heat and add the unsalted butter pieces, stirring until melted. The butter will thicken the sauce.

To Serve

Remove the foil from the chicken and ham and spoon the spinach and sauce over the top.

This dish needs to be served immediately.

Notes: Cook the chicken at the last minute otherwise it becomes dry and the dish is spoiled.

The sauce can be cooked during the day, reheated, but add the butter at the last moment, and then at dinner time you can add the spinach. This sauce can be used for other dishes. It is lovely over fillets of fish. Sauté the fish in butter first, in the same way as you do the chicken breasts for this dish.

INGREDIENTS
6 chicken breasts, boned (see page 60)
½ bunch spinach

SAUCE
1 cup (8 fl oz) dry white wine
1 cup (8 fl oz) chicken stock
½ cup (4 fl oz) pure cream
60 g (2 oz) unsalted butter

REMAINING INGREDIENTS
salt and pepper
60 g (2 oz) butter
6 slices ham

CHICKEN BREASTS

It is easy to buy chicken breasts although they are usually sold attached to the bones.

To bone a chicken breast should only take about 30 seconds. The bones which are left can be added to stock.

1. Using a sharp kitchen knife, remove the wing from the chicken breast.

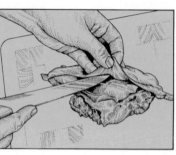

2. Pull the skin back. Make a cut straight down where the rib is located.

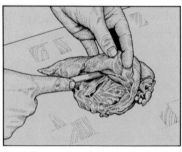

3. Pull very gently, scrape the flesh away from the bone.

4. Separate the bone from the meat. Pull out the white tendon.

CHICKEN BREASTS IN A CRUST

Remove the skin from the chicken breasts and bone them. Melt the butter in a frying pan and when foaming sauté the chicken breasts on both sides until they have changed colour. Do not overcook, they must still be very raw in the centre. Leave aside to cool. Season them.

Stuffing

Using a small sharp knife, cut all the flesh from the chicken legs, then cut this into small dice. Melt the butter in a frying pan and add the spring onions, diced mushrooms and a little salt and pepper. Cook a minute, stirring, then add the finely diced meat from the chicken legs.

Add the champagne or white wine and cook over high heat until this has all boiled away. During this time the chicken leg meat will cook in the wine. Then place this mixture into a bowl and add the crumbs, parsley, garlic and egg. Cut the additional 30 g (1 oz) butter into tiny pieces and add to the stuffing. Leave to become quite cold.

To Assemble

Place a slice of ham down on a board, put a generous mound of

INGREDIENTS

6 chicken breasts
45 g (1½ oz) butter
salt and pepper

STUFFING

3 chicken legs
45 g (1½ oz) butter
1 tablespoon spring onions, chopped
125 g (4 oz) mushrooms, diced small
salt and pepper
½ cup (4 fl oz) champagne or dry white wine
3 tablespoons breadcrumbs made from stale bread
1 tablespoon parsley, finely chopped
1 clove garlic, crushed
1 egg
an additional 30 g (1 oz) butter

60

stuffing on this and then top with one of the chicken breasts. Roll the puff pastry out very thinly. Cut into a piece slightly larger than double the size of the chicken breast and ham. Place the chicken and ham package on top of the pastry. Wrap the pastry over the top and then pinch the edges together. It will look rather like a pasty.

Beat the egg with the salt and brush the edges and top of the packages. Decorate with a cut-out of pastry if you wish. Prick the top once and then chill. These can be prepared about 12 hours beforehand.

To Cook

Place pasties on a buttered scone tray and cook in a moderately hot oven 200° C (425° F) for about 25-30 minutes. The chicken breasts will cook through during this time and the pastry become puffed and golden brown.

Serve plain or with the Mushroom and Champagne Sauce.

Mushroom and Champagne Sauce

Melt the butter and add the mushrooms. Season with salt and pepper and cook over high heat until they are just softened. Add the squeeze of lemon juice.

Add the champagne or white wine and the Madeira or sherry and cook until the pan is almost dry. Remove from the heat.

In a separate saucepan melt the additional butter and add the flour. Cook, stirring until the mixture is slightly granulated but do not let it brown. Add the chicken stock and bring to the boil, stirring constantly until the mixture is thickened. Then cook gently until it has thickened a little more and will coat the back of a spoon. This takes about 20 minutes.

Add the mushroom mixture and the cream and check for seasoning.

Note: This does have a rather unfortunate resemblance to a pasty in appearance, but it is the only logical way to wrap the chicken breasts.

TO ASSEMBLE
6 slices ham
750 g (1½ lb) puff pastry
1 egg
pinch salt

MUSHROOM AND CHAMPAGNE SAUCE
45 g (1½ oz) butter
125 g (4 oz) mushrooms
salt and pepper
squeeze lemon juice
½ cup (4 fl oz) champagne or dry white wine
2 tablespoons Madeira, or medium dry sherry
an additional 45 g (1½ oz) butter
2 tablespoons flour
2 cups (16 fl oz) chicken stock
3 tablespoons cream
salt and pepper as needed

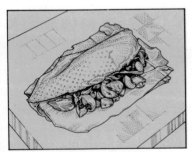

1. Place the ham and chicken on a thin square of puff pastry which is approximately double the size of the chicken breast.

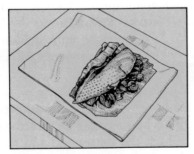

2. Cut the edge slightly to make more of an oval shape to the pastry and fold over, pinching the edges together firmly so it looks rather like a pasty.

STUFFED CHICKEN IN FILO

INGREDIENTS
6 chicken breasts

STUFFING
1 bunch spinach
salt
60 g (2 oz) butter
1 teaspoon curry powder
2 hard boiled eggs
45 g (1½ oz) ham, diced small
salt and pepper
45 g (1½ oz) butter

TO ASSEMBLE
30 g (1 oz) butter
filo pastry
additional butter

CHICKEN AND WHITE WINE SAUCE
45 g (1½ oz) butter
1 tablespoon and 2 teaspoons flour
½ cup (4 fl oz) dry white wine
¾ cup (6 fl oz) chicken stock
¼ cup (2 fl oz) cream

Remove the skin from the chicken breasts and bone them. Cut them through the centre to make a pocket.

Stuffing
Wash the spinach well and then just leave the water that is on the leaves. Place this into a large saucepan, add a little salt and cook, stirring occasionally until just tender, about 5 minutes. Do not overcook. Remove and drain and then squeeze or pat dry. Place the spinach down on a board and chop it roughly.

Melt the butter in a frying pan. Add the curry and fry for a few seconds, then add the spinach and cook, stirring until it is coated with butter and curry.

Mash the hard boiled eggs, mix in with the ham and a little salt and pepper. Remove from the heat and leave to cool.

Place a spoonful of the filling into the cavity of the chicken breast and press gently together. It sticks easily as the filling is quite moist.

To Cook the Chicken
Melt the butter in a frying pan. Add the chicken breasts and cook, turning carefully once until the outside is golden. The chicken will still be raw in the middle. Remove and leave to cool.

Wrapping in Filo
When handling filo, the remaining sheets should be kept covered with a damp piece of kitchen paper or a dampened tea towel to prevent drying. Some brands of filo have too much flour on the sheets. This can be brushed away using a dry pastry brush.

Place a sheet of filo down on the bench and cut it just slightly wider than the chicken breast. Melt some butter in a saucepan. Start with 45 g (1½ oz) and add more as you need it. Brush the filo with a pastry brush, coating well with butter. Place another sheet of filo on top. Butter this. Then place a chicken breast down one end and roll over. Do not tuck the ends in, this makes it too thick. Altogether you should have about 5 to 6 thicknesses of filo on the outside, but no more than this. Brush the outside with a little extra butter. Place on a lightly buttered scone tray and chill until you want to cook them.

Place in moderate oven 180-190° C (350-375° F) for about 20 to 25 minutes or until golden brown and crisp. During this cooking time the chicken will cook in the centre.

Chicken and Wine Sauce
Although the stuffing is quite moist sometimes filo can be a little dry. This sauce can be served on the table with the dish.

Melt the butter and add the flour. Cook, stirring until the flour is slightly granulated but don't let it brown. Add the white wine and chicken stock and stir until the sauce comes to the boil. It will be rather thin at this stage. Cook, uncovered for about 20 minutes or until it coats the back of a spoon. Add the cream. Season and then cook a few minutes longer. This sauce can be made beforehand and then reheated more successfully.

Notes: This dish can be prepared about 4 or 5 hours beforehand and kept refrigerated until ready to cook.

When you wrap the filo around the chicken, although it isn't necessary to tuck the ends in, make sure that the filo is slightly wider than the chicken, if the breast of chicken is outside, the edges will become dry when cooked. The filo protects the chicken meat, so it remains moist.

1. Cut the chicken breasts at the thickest side to form a pocket.

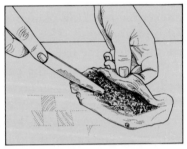

2. Fill the pocket with stuffing and press edges of chicken together gently.

3. Cut filo, brush with melted butter and place a second piece on top.

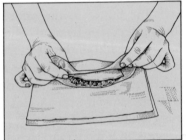

4. Place the chicken breast on the filo and turn over to form a roll.

DUCK

Duck has a higher proportion of bone and leg meat than a chicken of the same weight so one duck will serve only four people, even if you only give them rather small portions.

When you cook duck, the breast meat will always be ready before the legs, so you either have to eat the breast a little well done, or the legs pink, which most people find unpleasant.

The French cook and serve their ducks to perfection in top restaurants by serving the breast when it is just ready. While you eat the breast, the legs are returned to the kitchen and cooked a little longer. You then eat the legs, generally with a little salad.

Ducks are easiest to buy frozen. Be sure to let them thaw completely before cooking and wash them well. Remove the wing joints and keep with the giblets to make some stock.

Pull out all the loose fat from inside the cavity and remove the neck and cut the little fat glands at the base of the tail area.

Because duck has a thick layer of fat under the skin which needs to be released during cooking, prick the skin of the duck all over, along the thighs and the back and then over the breast.

FESTIVAL CHICKEN

INGREDIENTS

1 chicken, 1.5 kg (3 lb)
salt cnd pepper
mango chutney
¼ fresh paw paw (or equivalent fruit)
2 tablespoons oil

SAUCE

30 g (1 oz) butter
1 medium-sized white onion, finely diced
2 ripe tomatoes about 375 g (12 oz)
1 flat tablespoon mild curry powder
¼ teaspoon salt
1 teaspoon mango chutney
½ cup (4 fl oz) cream
1 tablespoon flaked almonds, lightly
*   browned in a dry pan*

In this chicken dish fruit is placed in the centre of the bird which is then cooked in a very light curry sauce. I use paw paw but actually any fresh fruit in season could be used. Never use tinned fruit because the entire dish becomes too sweet.

You could try pineapple, fresh apricots or peaches in season.

Remove the fatty portions from the tail of the chicken and then cut off the wing tips and remove the neck if it is still inside. Season the chicken with salt and pepper. Spread the inside of the chicken with a little mango chutney. You can use a spoon to spread this around. This is not so much to flavour the chicken but to flavour the paw paw.

Remove the skin of the paw paw and scoop away the dark seeds. Cut the paw paw into long pieces and push these into the cavity of the chicken. Then tie or truss the chicken. Heat the oil in a pan and brown the chicken on all sides. Keep it moving so it will not stick. Remove the chicken and tip out the oil from the pan before beginning the sauce.

Sauce

Melt the butter in the same pan. Add the onion and sauté, stirring occasionally until softened. Cut the tomatoes into rough pieces and add to the pan together with the curry powder and salt. Stir for a few minutes to fry the curry. Place the vegetables in a casserole that has a tight fitting lid. Place the chicken on top of them. Cover with the lid. The chicken and paw paw will make quite a bit of liquid.

Cook in a moderate oven 180-190° C (350-375° F) until the chicken is tender, approximately 1 hour to 1 hour and 10 minutes should be long enough. There is no need to baste or turn the chicken.

Remove the casserole from the oven and take out the chicken. Keep warm on the side. Strain the juices from the casserole into a saucepan. Push down to get all the juice from the tomato, etc. Add the chutney and cream and boil rapidly until it forms a thick sauce. This will only take a few minutes. Add the flaked almonds to the sauce.

To Serve

Carve the chicken into portions and arrange on a platter. Coat with the sauce. Remove the paw paw from the centre (it will be quite soft) and arrange this on the side of the platter. Serve a little portion of the paw paw with each piece of chicken.

DUCK WITH SOUR CHERRY SAUCE

A slightly sweet and sour duck recipe. It is essential to use the sour cherries which you can buy either in a jar or tin, usually these are already stoned. The cherries we have in Australia are too sweet and should not be used for this type of dish.

Remove the fat from the tail of the duck. Salt the duck. Remove lower wing part. Truss the duck. Prick the skin around the thighs, back and lower breast using a sharp fork. Place the water in a baking tin. Then put the duck in the tin, breast side up. Put into a moderately hot oven, 200° C (425° F) for about 15 minutes. Then turn the oven down to moderate, 180-190° C (350-375° F) and turn the duck on one side. Cook, pricking occasionally so the fat will be released. After about 30 minutes on one side, turn the duck over onto the other side. The skin will be lovely and crisp, the flesh tender. It usually takes from 1¼ to 1½ hours but can vary.

While the duck is cooking make up the sauce. Place the sugar and vinegar in a small saucepan and cook over low heat until the sugar is dissolved. Then turn up the heat and cook more rapidly until the mixture is becoming a golden brown. Add the chicken stock and simmer to dissolve the little hard bits of caramel that will form.

Mix the cornflour with just a little water and add to the stock. Simmer gently for about 10 minutes. Leave aside.

Place the drained sour cherries in a bowl, add the brandy and orange juice. Stand for about 1 hour. Mix these with the sauce.

To Assemble and Serve

Remove the duck from the oven and discard the trussing strings. Place on a platter and leave in a warm oven with the door ajar. Try to remove as much fat as you can from the pan, leaving any juice behind. Usually this is difficult and I just tip out everything in the dish otherwise the sauce becomes fatty and unpleasant.

Place the pan on the heat and add about ¼ cup water. While heating stir and scrape up all the little brown bits on the base. Pour this little bit of liquid through a strainer and add to the cherry sauce. Heat the cherry sauce again, adding the red currant jelly which takes just a few minutes to dissolve.

Check the seasoning. The taste should be just slightly sweet. If it is too sweet a little lemon could be added.

Carve the duck, remove the leg and then the wing. Then set the duck on its back and cut down along each side of the breast bone and remove the entire breast from each side. Place this on a board and cut the breast in thin, long slices.

Arrange the slices of breast in the centre of a platter and the wing and leg portions down the ends. Cover with a little of the sauce and then serve the remainder in a jug on the table.

Notes: With this type of dish, the sauce and cherries have a special flavour which doesn't seem to go particularly well with vegetables. Shoestring or simple round potatoes cooked in a little butter are the best choice as an accompaniment.

INGREDIENTS
1 duck 2 kg (4 lb)
salt
½ cup (4 fl oz) water

SAUCE
1 tablespoon sugar
2 tablespoons white vinegar
1½ cups (12 fl oz) chicken stock
1 tablespoon cornflour
½ cup (4 oz) sour cherries, stoned
2 tablespoons brandy
⅓ cup (2½ fl oz) orange juice
¼ cup water
1 tablespoon red currant jelly

SUNFLOWER CHICKEN

INGREDIENTS

6 chicken breasts, boned
60 g (2 oz) butter
2 tablespoons spring onion, finely chopped
1 green apple, peeled and diced
½ cup (4 fl oz) thick or pure cream

MARINADE

1½ cups (12 fl oz) dry white wine
4 tablespoons port
1 tablespoon Saté spice (sometimes called Gado Gado)
good pinch salt

SUNFLOWER SEEDS

⅓ cup (2 oz) sunflower seeds
1 cup (8 fl oz) chicken stock

Sunflower seeds can be bought in health food shops and are an interesting combination with chicken but must be cooked first or they taste like little rocks in the dish. They have a lovely nutty flavour and an unusual texture when correctly prepared.

Flatten the chicken breasts between some paper until they are of an even thickness. Mix the ingredients for the marinade in a glass or china bowl and add the chicken breasts. Leave to stand for about 30 minutes to 1 hour but no longer. Remove and drain. Place the sunflower seeds in a saucepan. Cover with water and bring to the boil. Remove from the heat and leave them to stand in the water for about 10 minutes. Drain.

Place them in the saucepan and cover with the cup of chicken stock. Bring to the boil and simmer very gently for another 10 minutes. Drain but keep the chicken stock as it will be used in the sauce.

Melt the butter in a large frying pan. Add the drained chicken breasts and cook on both sides until golden. This should only take a couple of minutes. Remove them from the pan. Add the spring onions and apple to the pan and cook until just tender. Remove these.

Add the marinade and chicken stock in which you cooked the sunflower seeds and cook over high heat until the mixture has gone down to about ¾ of a cup. It doesn't take long in a frying pan because of the wide surface. Add the cream, cook a little longer until the mixture has thickened and lightly coats a spoon.

Return the chicken breasts to the pan and spoon the liquid over them. Add spring onion and apple and cook a few minutes longer, then scatter the sunflower seeds over the top and just let them heat through.

Notes: This dish can be partly prepared beforehand. You can sauté the chicken breasts, cook the apple and spring onion and prepare the sauce. Then reheat the sauce and add the chicken to reheat. Once cooked however, the chicken breasts are best served almost immediately.

If you don't like quite so many sunflower seeds you can cut the quantity by half.

You may notice that there is only a pinch of salt in the marinade. By the time it is cooked down and reduced to ¾ cup this will have become quite well seasoned so do not be tempted to add more unless you taste at the finish and decide you want more salt.

Because this book is a collection of the most popular recipes from the cooking school the meats are mainly more expensive cuts which are used for special dinners.

There are some recipes, such as the lamb chops, legs of lamb, a minced beef and a veal recipe which are more inexpensive but on the whole the meats are the better quality pieces.

LAMB KIDNEYS IN ANCHOVY SAUCE

Probably one of the most commonly eaten kidneys in Australia would be lamb kidneys, which are small and dark and shaped like a large bean. Occasionally they can have a strong taste but if you prepare them this way, any strong taste of ammonia will disappear. The outside membrane of these kidneys and the little firm section of fat which is on the inside should be removed.

Check that the kidneys are well trimmed. Melt the unsalted butter in a frying pan. Add the kidneys and then cook on both sides for a couple of minutes until they have changed colour. Remove the kidneys to a sieve and place over a basin. Leave to stand for about 15 to 20 minutes and during this time quite a lot of blood will drip away. This leaves the kidneys much sweeter in flavour as the blood has a strong ammonia flavour. Discard the blood and lightly rinse the kidneys in a bowl of cold water. Leave aside to drain on kitchen paper.

To the butter in the pan, add garlic and spring onions and cook for a minute, then add the wine and chicken stock. Boil rapidly until reduced. It will not make a very thick sauce but should cook down to about half.

Mash the anchovies well. Add to the sauce.

Next, slice the kidneys across, removing the centre core. Add the kidneys to the pan and cook gently to heat them through and cook a little more in the centre. This will only take a moment. Remove the pan from the heat.

Add the unsalted butter to the sauce and stir until it melts. It shouldn't need salt but you can add a little pepper if you wish.

Serve immediately.

Notes: This type of dish is good with a pilaf of rice or toast fingers. It is fairly pungent in flavour because of the anchovies. If you wish, the dish can be prepared beforehand, up to adding the sliced kidneys, and then reheated later in the day. Be careful not to overcook the kidneys. Unsalted butter is used because the anchovies are so salty.

INGREDIENTS

12 lamb kidneys
30 g (1 oz) unsalted butter
1 clove garlic, crushed
1 tablesoon spring onions, finely diced
1 cup (8 fl oz) red wine
¼ cup (2 fl oz) chicken stock
1 x 45 g (1½ oz) tin flat anchovy fillets

TO FINISH

30 g (1 oz) unsalted butter

LAMB CHOPS WITH PARSLEY AND BACON STUFFING

INGREDIENTS
6 lamb chops, cut very thick
a little black pepper

FILLING
125 g (4 oz) bacon
2 cloves, garlic, crushed
½ cup (¾ oz) parsley, finely chopped

TO COOK
1 tablespoon oil
toothpicks

SAUCE
½ cup (4 fl oz) dry white wine
½ cup (4 fl oz) chicken stock
2 teaspoons Worcestershire sauce
2 tablespoons parsley, finely chopped
salt and pepper
30 g (1 oz) butter, cut into pieces

The lamb chops which are already cut by the butcher will be too thin for this dish. You need to have them cut especially. They should be at least 4 cm (1½ in) thick.

Middle loin chops are the best. One chop per person should be sufficient but you can allow more if you wish.

Remove some of the fat from the lamb and then cut from the outside to make a pocket. Cut right through to the bone. Open this out and season with some pepper. No salt is needed, as the bacon is sufficiently salty.

Filling
Dice the bacon into small pieces. Mix with the crushed garlic and chopped parsley. Place a spoonful of this filling inside the chops. Press together. Hold with a small wooden toothpick. The tail part of the chop can be wrapped around and secured also.

To Cook
Brush the outside of the chops with a little oil. Place on a baking tray and cook in a moderately hot oven 220° C (425° F) for about 12 to 15 minutes or until just cooked. Timing really depends on the thickness of the chops. The meat should be slightly pink in the centre when served.

Sauce
Place the white wine and chicken stock in a saucepan and cook rapidly until reduced by half. Then add the Worcestershire sauce, parsley and season with salt and pepper. Remove from the heat. Add the butter, one piece at a time at the last moment, off the heat. This will glaze and lightly thicken the sauce.

Notes: This is not really so much a sauce as a light juice served with the chops. If you wish to have a thicker sauce, mix a couple of teaspoons of cornflour mixed with stock in with the sauce at the finish.

Do not forget to remove the toothpicks before serving.

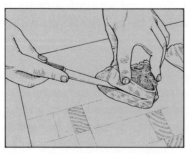

1. Cut each lamb chop through to the bone to form a pocket.

2. Insert a spoonful of the bacon filling into each pocket.

LEG OF LAMB BAKED WITH SPINACH

The lamb is partly cooked and then layered with spinach between the slices. As it is partly boned it is quite easy to carve. This is a most interesting dish in both looks and flavour.

If the lamb is very fatty trim a little of this from the top. Cut the garlic into thin slivers. Using a sharp knife cut some slashes in the meat near the bone. Stud each one with a piece of garlic.

Place the lamb directly on the oven rack and bake at 180-190° C (350-375° F). Place a dish underneath to catch the fat. This dish can have a little water placed in it to stop the fat spluttering. Cook for 1 hour for very pink meat, 1 hour 20 minutes for slightly well done meat which will have a pink tinge at the bone.

Remove and leave to cool for at least 30 minutes.

After the lamb is cooked and cooled, cut the shank bone through at the end. This needs to be left on while the lamb is cooking as the meat will stay moist this way.

Cut the meat into diagonal slices. There should be about 12 slices altogether.

Spinach Filling

Melt the butter in a saucepan. Add the onions and cook, stirring occasionally until softened and just barely golden. Add the flour and cook to fry for a few minutes. Add the milk and cook, stirring constantly until it comes to the boil. Season with nutmeg, mustard, salt and pepper.

In another saucepan cook the frozen spinach until soft. Leave the lid off the saucepan so it will be fairly dry. When cooked remove and drain really well. Add this spinach to the sauce and then push the entire mixture through a sieve. Leave to cool as it is much easier to handle cold. If it appears too liquid then cook again over the heat, stirring to thicken a little.

Place a little of the spinach filling on each slice of lamb. Cut the ham squares or circles into halves and place one of these over the spinach. Continue covering all the slices of meat. Keep enough filling over to spread a few spoonfuls over the lamb.

Topping

Mix the crumbs and cheese together and sprinkle over the top.

Keep refrigerated until you wish to bake the meat, but let it return to room temperature before baking.

To Cook

Place in a baking tin in a moderate oven, 180-190° C (350-375° F) for 30 minutes. The top will become golden brown and the filling will heat through. The meat can be cooked a little longer if you wish, but you may need to place a piece of foil on top.

When you serve loosen the slices with a knife and then cut them level with the bone. They will lift out easily.

INGREDIENTS
1 leg lamb, 1.5 kg (3 to 3½ lb)
1 large clove garlic

SPINACH FILLING
60 g (2 oz) butter
2 white onions, finely diced
1 tablespoon flour
1 cup (8 fl oz) milk
pinch nutmeg
1 teaspoon dry, English-style mustard
salt and pepper
1 packet frozen spinach, 290 g (9 oz)
6 square or round slices of ham

TOPPING
3 tablespoons breadcrumbs made from stale bread
3 tablespoons parmesan cheese, finely grated

VEAL WITH TWO SAUCES

This is a dish of veal paupiettes which are filled with minced veal and pork. The quantity of minced meat is rather small so you really need to have either your own mincer or a food processor. It is served with the two sauces which gives an unusual and attractive appearance, with the white sauce on one side and the pink tomato sauce on the other.

Place the veal between waxed paper and beat out until it is thin.

Mix the minced veal, pork, bacon, garlic, salt, pepper and nutmeg in a basin. Make this into 6 little sausage shapes. Place one on each slice of veal, down the end. Roll over, tucking in the ends to make a little cigar shape. Tie these rolls in at least two places. If they are large you may need three pieces of string.

Heat the butter and oil in a frying pan. Cook the veal over medium heat on the outside, turning until it is golden.

Transfer the veal, the butter and oil to a casserole with a lid. Cook in the oven for another 15 minutes or so until quite tender and the filling in the centre has cooked through.

Remove from the oven. Place the veal on a platter.

Spoon the cheese sauce carefully on one side of the dish. Spoon the tomato sauce carefully over the other side.

Serve immediately.

INGREDIENTS

VEAL

6 slices leg veal, cut very thinly as for schnitzel

FILLING FOR VEAL

60 g (2 oz) veal, minced
375 g (6 oz) pork, minced
1 rasher bacon, diced small
1 clove garlic, crushed
½ teaspoon salt
a little white pepper
½ teaspoon grated nutmeg

TO COOK THE VEAL

30 g (1 oz) butter
1 tablespoon oil

CHEESE SAUCE

60 g (2 oz) butter
1 tablespoon flour
1 cup (8 fl oz) milk
30 g (1 oz) gruyère cheese, grated
salt and pepper

TOMATO SAUCE

60 g (2 oz) butter
1 white onion, finely diced
1 clove garlic, crushed
1 tablespoon plain flour
2 ripe tomatoes, 375 g (12 oz)
salt and pepper
little sugar if needed
½ cup (4 fl oz) red wine

Cheese Sauce

Melt the butter and add the flour. Cook for a few minutes until the flour is granulated. Add the milk and bring to the boil, stirring constantly. Cook for a couple of minutes.

Add the cheese, remove immediately from the heat and stir until the cheese melts. Season with salt and pepper.

Tomato Sauce

Melt the butter in a saucepan and add the onion. Sauté, stirring occasionally until the onion is softened. Add the garlic and flour and fry for a few minutes until the flour is cooked.

Cut the tomatoes into rough pieces and add to the pan with salt, pepper, a little sugar if the tomatoes are tart, and red wine. Cook until this mixture has come to the boil, stir well.

Cover the pan and simmer gently for about 20 minutes. Push through a sieve or moulin.

Notes: This dish may look involved but many parts can be done well beforehand. The veal can be prepared and kept refrigerated and then browned later in the day. You can leave it in the casserole ready for cooking.

The cheese sauce can be made, but don't add the gruyère or the cheese spoils. Make the sauce and then warm gently again, then add the cheese. If it becomes too thick when you reheat you can thin with a little cream.

The tomato sauce can be made beforehand and keeps refrigerated for several days.

This dish is good served with noodles and particularly good with green tagliatelle as a base.

FILLET OF BEEF

The most tender of all meats, a fillet, is surrounded by a casing of fat, sinews and some gristle. Because of the high cost of this meat many people don't feel they want to trim away all the casing but I really think this is essential. Otherwise the finished dish has a firm outside casing and can sometimes be chewy.

If you can't afford to buy fillet, then it's much more sensible to buy a cheaper but tasty piece of meat and serve a different dish altogether.

To Trim

Cut away and pull off any fat on the outside of the meat. There is a long thin piece of meat along one side of the fillet. Pull or cut this away.

Cut the large lumps of fat out from the side.

Remove the shiny sinew on top of the meat and pull until it is all away. The meat should look quite clean and the narrow little bit of the tail can be tucked under and tied. Tie the fillet in several places to hold a good shape if cooking it whole.

The beef that is sold over the counter is usually from young animals and the fillets are small and narrow. Your timing for cooking the beef should depend more on thickness than on weight. A long, thin fillet will take less time to cook than the same weight of fillet which is short and fat.

The meat is cooked when it has lost its softness and becomes resilient to the touch.

Always allow the finished fillet to rest, covered lightly with some foil in a warm place, for 5 minutes before carving.

TO COOK YOUNG, THIN FILLETS OF BEEF, ALLOW:

10 minutes per 500 g (1 lb) for very rare
12 minutes per 500 g (1 lb) for medium
15 minutes per 500 g (1 lb) for well done

TO COOK SHORT, FAT FILLETS OF BEEF, ALLOW:

14 minutes per 500 g (1 lb) for very rare
16 minutes per 500 g (1 lb) for medium
18 minutes per 500 g (1 lb) for well done

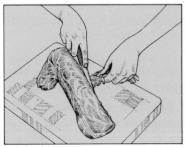

1. With a sharp knife remove the fat from the fillet and also the "chain" from the side which contains gristle.

2. Using kitchen paper towelling so the meat won't slip, remove the thin, layer of sinew on top which covers the meat.

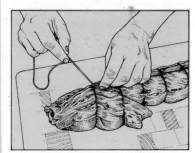

3. Fold the narrow tail section underneath and tie with string so it will retain a good shape when cooked.

71

FILLET RENÉ VERDON

INGREDIENTS
1.25 kg (2½-3 lb) fillet of beef
1 tablespoon oil

ESCARGOT BUTTER
1 tablespoon shallots, chopped
2 tablespoons dry white wine
125 g (4 oz) butter
1 tablespoon parsley, finely chopped
2 cloves garlic, crushed
salt and pepper
3 tablespoons breadcrumbs
¼ cup (1 oz) gruyère cheese, grated

During the Kennedy administration in the USA a chef was chosen to elevate the standard of cooking at the White House. The chef was René Verdon, a tall, large man with a warm smile and an ebullient personality who now owns a restaurant in San Francisco called 'Le Trianon'.

He gave me an excellent recipe for escargot butter and I have used this butter between thin slices of fillet steak and named the dish Fillet René Verdon after this well-known chef. The butter melts as the steak is cooked, flavouring the meat and giving it a wonderful moistness.

Place the shallots and white wine in a small saucepan. Cook over a moderate heat until the white wine has almost evaporated away and the shallots are soft.

Cream the butter with the parsley, garlic, salt, pepper and add the breadcrumbs and cheese. Mix in the shallots.

To Prepare Meat
Trim the beef. Heat the oil in a frying pan and when very hot add the beef. Turn on all sides until it is brown on the outside.

Remove the beef and leave to cool. Cut the beef into thinnish slices leaving it attached at the base. The slices should be barely 1 cm (½ in) thick.

Spread some of the butter between every slice and retain about a tablespoon to spread on the sides and top of the beef.

Tie string around the beef to hold it together.

Place the beef on an ungreased tray with edges or in a dish. Bake in moderate oven (not hot as is usual, or the butter will go brown). Cook, according to the thickness of the beef.

Remove, let stand for 5 to 10 minutes with some foil over the top. Remove the string and then cut the slices through.

Note: There will be a lot of butter on the tray; some stays between the beef, some will melt out. This butter can be spooned over the beef just before you cut it and then any of the remaining butter can be kept. Refrigerate to firm it. You can spread a little on chops or potatoes.

1. *Cut the beef, three-quarters of the way down, into thin slices leaving it attached at the base.*

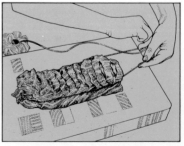

2. *Spread the butter between these slices, then tie the fillet horizontally to keep the slices in place while cooking.*

Roasted Steak with Onions (page 77)

LAMB IN A SALT CRUST

The salt crust is used as a method of cooking. It keeps the meat very moist and flavours it lightly on the outside. Although the crust looks lovely and brown and tempting to eat, it tastes terrible, and don't nibble it or you will be thirsty for hours afterwards! Have the butcher bone the lamb but ask him to leave the shank end in. Also request that he does not cut the shank as usual. By having the bone straight it makes the lamb easier to handle.

If the lamb is very fatty cut away some of the outside fat. Heat the oil in a frying pan and add the lamb. Brown on the outside, turning until it is a good colour on all sides. Leave to cool.

Crust

Mix the dry ingredients together. Mix the water with the oil and stir into the dry ingredients. Mix and knead lightly with your fingers to form a dough. Place back in the basin, or on a bench and cover with a damp tea towel. Leave for 10 minutes. This makes it easier to roll. Roll out to make an oval shape which is a little larger than the meat.

Place the meat on the centre of the crust and wrap over. Place the join underneath and put lamb onto a greased baking dish. Chill for 30 minutes.

Place the lamb in a moderate oven 180-190° C (350-375° F) and bake for 1½ hours. Remove from the oven and leave to stand for at least 10 minutes or longer. The lamb will have just a slight tinge of pink at the centre.

To Carve

The crust will feel rather solid. You need a small kitchen saw or a large sharp knife to open it easily. Cut into the crust at one end and cut a line straight down the centre. Then insert your fingers into this hole and part the two sections a little. The crust will come away easily once you have done this. The meat will be very hot inside the crust so be careful the steam doesn't burn you.

For effect this should be taken to the table with the crust just slightly cut and then this can be removed before carving. To cut the crust requires quite a strong hand so it's best not to attempt the entire thing in the dining room.

Note: If you have chilled the lamb for longer than 30 minutes the meat will be very cold and so add another 10 or 15 minutes to the cooking time.

INGREDIENTS
1 leg lamb 1.5 kg (3 to 3½ lb)
1 tablespoon oil

SALT CRUST
3½ cups (14 oz) flour
½ cup (2 oz) self-raising flour
¾ cup (6 oz) salt
1⅓ cups (10 fl oz) water
2 tablespoons oil

Three Star Fillet (page 82)

RACKS OF LAMB 'FRENCH STYLE'

INGREDIENTS

2 racks or 2 loins lamb
1 large clove garlic, cut into thin slivers
30 g (1 oz) butter

SAUCE

30 g (1 oz) butter
1 medium-sized onion, diced small
1 medium-sized carrot, diced
1 clove garlic, crushed
1 tablespoon flour
125 g (4 oz) mushrooms, thinly sliced
½ cup (4 fl oz) red wine
1½ cups (12 fl oz) chicken stock
salt and pepper
bouquet garni of a large sprig of parsley,
  mint and thyme

GARNISH

1 large ripe tomato, peeled
1 teaspoon mint, finely chopped

You can prepare this dish with either two racks of lamb of about seven to eight chops or small loins.

The loins must be trimmed of some of the fat so they do not make the sauce too fatty, and it is easiest if loins are boned first and then tied.

Using a sharp knife cut little slits between every bone of the rack or at intervals down the loin. Place a small piece of garlic in these slits. Heat the butter in a frying pan and add the lamb, fat side down. Cook for a few minutes until a good golden brown colour. Remove.

Sauce

Melt the butter and add the onion and carrot. Sauté gently, stirring occasionally until the onion is softened. Add the garlic and flour and fry for a few minutes. Add the mushrooms, red wine, stock, a little salt and pepper if needed and bring to the boil, stirring constantly. Add the bouquet garni.

Pour this sauce into the base of a casserole with deep sides. It is not cooked with a lid but if the dish is too shallow the sauce will evaporate too quickly. Place the lamb on top of the sauce.

Bake in a moderate oven 180-190° C (350-375° F) for 1 hour or until the lamb is just slightly pink. This really depends on the time of year for the lamb. During this cooking the sauce will reduce a little.

Garnish

Cut the tomato into quarters and squeeze gently to remove some of the seeds. Cut the flesh into little pieces. Mix with the mint.

Remove the lamb from the sauce. Pour the sauce through a strainer. Return to a saucepan and add the tomato strips and mint. If too thin, cook rapidly for a few minutes.

Cut the lamb into slices and arrange overlapping on a plate. Spoon just a little of the sauce over the top and serve the remainder on the table in a jug. The sauce should be checked for seasoning and it occasionally needs a pinch of sugar to bring out the flavourings.

Notes: This can be prepared to a certain stage beforehand. The lamb can be browned hours before and the sauce made well in advance. However, keep them separate until you are ready to cook them.

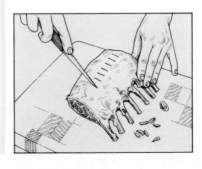

1. Using a small sharp knife cut slits between each bone on the rack of lamb, large enough for a sliver of garlic to be inserted.

ROASTED STEAK WITH ONION

I generally use a good quality piece of steak such as rump for this dish. If you use a cheaper cut you will need to alter the timing to allow for this.

Make small slashes through the fat on the side of the steak. Cut the onions into thickish slices. Place them on the steak to cover the outside and have the fat portion of the steak as the base. Use the toothpicks to secure the onions. They will shrink a little as they cook so you can even overlap them a little. They will become nicely coloured and flavour the meat.

Place this meat on a lightly oiled tray in the oven. Cook in a moderately hot oven, 200° C (425° F). The timing is difficult to give as it really depends on whether the steak has been cut as a fat piece or as a longer thinner slab. It can vary from 35 minutes to 45 minutes.

Sauce

While the steak is cooking the sauce can be prepared. Place the red wine, beef stock and spring onions in a small saucepan and cook until it has been reduced by half. When the steak is ready, take it from the oven and remove the onions. Leave the steak aside for about 10 minutes.

The onions will still be a little firm. Add them to the sauce and leave them to cook. During this time the sauce will reduce a little more. Taste for salt and pepper. Remove from heat.

Before serving, cut the butter into small pieces and add to the sauce. This will make it glossy and give it extra richness.

To Serve

Cut the beef into thin slices. Serve topped with some of the sauce and onions.

Notes: We have often made this dish using a commercial beef consommé and found it most successful. It can become a little salty, however, so be careful of seasoning the sauce until you taste, and use an unsalted butter at the finish.

INGREDIENTS

*1 thick piece of rump steak 1.25 kg
   (2½-3 lb)
2 or 3 large white onions
toothpicks*

SAUCE

*1 cup (8 fl oz) red wine
1 cup (8 fl oz) beef stock
1 tablespoon spring onions, finely chopped
salt and pepper
30 g (1 oz) butter*

Overlapping them slightly, place onion rings all over the steak. Secure with toothpicks.

BEEF WITH PICKLED WALNUTS

INGREDIENTS
12 thin slices fillet of beef, trimmed well
45 g (1½ oz) butter
2 teaspoons oil
a little black pepper
salt

SAUCE
2 tablespoons shallots, chopped
1 cup (8 fl oz) beef stock
1 cup (8 fl oz) red wine
2 tablespoons brandy
½ cup (4 fl oz) pure cream
4 to 5 pickled walnuts

This is a dish which is cooked very quickly with little preparation. Pickled walnuts are rarely used in cooking. They are mainly served with cheeses at the finish of a meal. They have an interesting, slightly sharp flavour which goes well with beef. You can buy them in most large stores or gourmet delicatessens.

Heat the butter and oil in a frying pan. If the pan won't hold all the beef at once, cook in two batches. When very hot add the beef slices, sauté on one side until the beef has just changed colour, turn and sauté on the other. The beef should still be rather raw in the middle at this stage. Remove and leave aside.

Before adding to the sauce the beef is seasoned with a little salt and some pepper.

Sauce
Add the shallots to the same pan and sauté for a minute. Add beef stock, red wine, brandy and cream. Boil rapidly until the sauce has reduced considerably and is thickened enough to lightly coat a wooden spoon.

Cut the pickled walnuts into slices.

Place the beef in the sauce and turn to coat each slice. Sprinkle the pickled walnuts over the top and leave the beef to cook for a couple of minutes. It is nicest if you serve it still pink in the centre.

Notes: Although this dish is quite simple to cook, you may sauté the beef during the day and make the sauce. The sauce then needs reheating and the beef can be added with the pickled walnuts.

Pickled walnuts have a dark, almost black outside when you take them from the liquid. This outside, which is actually the shell, is quite soft and has a rather unattractive appearance. Using a piece of paper towelling you can gently rub this away. Once or twice I have found a pickled walnut in the jars which has been picked a little late and is very hard. Any walnut like this should be discarded. Normally pickled walnuts are as soft as ripe fruit. All the liquid must be drained from each piece before using as it is too sharp. Once opened, the jar of walnuts keeps for months in a cool place.

CAPER SAUCE

This sauce can be served with any large roasted piece of lamb and is particularly good with the lamb in the salt crust.

Melt the butter and add the flour. Fry, stirring until the flour is granulated. Add the milk and chicken stock and cook, stirring until it comes to the boil.

Mix the tomato paste and mustard with a teaspoon of the hot liquid. Add this mixture to the sauce and cook gently for about 10 minutes. It should just coat the back of a spoon.

Then mix together the egg yolk and cream. Mix some of the hot liquid into this and return to the heat. Don't let it boil once the egg is added, keep warm. Add the capers just before serving.

INGREDIENTS
30 g (1 oz) butter
2 teaspoons flour
½ cup (4 fl oz) milk
½ cup (4 fl oz) chicken stock
1 teaspoon tomato paste
1 teaspoon dry, English-style mustard
2 tablespoons capers, halved if large
1 egg yolk
¼ cup (2 fl oz) cream

MARINATED LAMB 'STANFORD COURT'

Fournou's Ovens restaurant is a part of the Stanford Court Hotel in San Francisco and yet an entity in its own right with a separate access to Nob Hill. The restaurant has big ovens faced in French provincial tiles, which are heated by oak and the specialties are the roasted meats baked in these ovens. It is an old fashioned method of cooking which gives beautifully crisp outside crusts on the meats and very moist tender meat inside. It cannot be duplicated in a home kitchen but the marinade which they use for the lamb can.

This marinade could be used for most pieces of roasting lamb. Mix all the marinade ingredients in a china bowl.
Have the racks trimmed by the butcher. If there is still excess fat, remove some of this from the top of the meat.

Using a small sharp knife, score across the back of the rack to make a diamond pattern. Place the racks in the marinade and leave to stand for 24 hours. You need to mix them around so the underneath ones are turned to the top of the marinade. It is easiest if the lamb is in a shallow bowl or container. Unless the weather is very hot they can be kept in a cool place to marinate. In hot weather the lamb must be refrigerated.

To Cook

Remove from the marinade and pat dry. Wrap foil around the bones to prevent charring. Place in hot oven 200° C (425° F), directly on the shelf. Put a dish underneath to catch any drips and have the top of the rack upwards. Time will vary according to how young the lamb is but calculate approximately: 25 minutes for rare: 30 minutes for medium: 35 for well done.

Notes: These can be served just plain as the marinade will have flavoured the meat. At Stanford Court Restaurant they serve a sauce, but I don't as a rule. Although I have given a timing for well done meat it spoils the meat if you serve racks of lamb well done. They should be sweet and slightly pink on the bone.

INGREDIENTS
6 racks of baby lamb, each of about 4 chops

MARINADE
1 white onion, finely diced
1 garlic clove, crushed
1 medium-sized carrot, diced
1 cup (8 fl oz) red wine
½ cup (4 fl oz) dry white wine
1 tablespoon tomato paste
large sprig parsley
1 bay leaf
a little rosemary
¼ teaspoon salt
pepper
good pinch tarragon

PEPPERCORN BEEF

INGREDIENTS

1 whole fillet of beef, 1.5 kg (3 lb) before trimming
black peppercorns

SAUCE

30 g (1 oz) butter
1 bunch spring onions, about ½ cup (2 oz) diced
1 clove garlic, crushed
1 cup (8 fl oz) beef stock
2 teaspoons tomato paste
¼ cup (2 fl oz) brandy
30 g (1 oz) unsalted butter, cut in small pieces

It is usual when cooking beef with peppercorns to cut the fillet into individual steaks and press peppercorns onto both sides. This beef has the peppercorns around the entire fillet. It still has the pepper flavour but it isn't quite so hot and strong as the usual peppercorn beef dishes.

Trim the beef and pull the skin away. Trim the fat and casing.

Using a small sharp knife, lightly cut little diamond patterns on the surface of the fillet.

Either crush some black peppercorns, or use a coarse grinder. Place a sheet of greaseproof paper down on a bench and spread a layer of the black peppercorns over this. It is often easiest to just grind them all over the paper. If you don't want this too hot, only have a light layer; if you like really hot pepper steak have a fairly solid layer.

Place the beef on the paper and roll over so all the sides are coated. The peppercorns will stick easily. Leave aside at room temperature for a couple of hours.

To Cook

Oil a baking tin. Have the oven on hot, 200-220° C (425-450° F). Cook the beef in the tin according to the thickness of the fillet.

Leave to stand for about 10 minutes to rest. Cut into slices and serve with the sauce.

Sauce

Melt the butter in a small saucepan and add the spring onions. Cook until just slightly softened. Add the garlic, beef stock, tomato paste and brandy. Boil rapidly until it has been reduced by at least half. This won't be a thick sauce but it has a nice glaze. Remove from the heat.

Just before serving, warm again, add the little pieces of butter one at a time and mix them in until melted. This gives the sauce a sheen and thickens it slightly.

Serve in a jug on the table with the beef.

Notes: This sauce shouldn't need any additional seasonings as by cooking down, saltiness is increased. It can be kept for several days, but don't add the butter until serving.

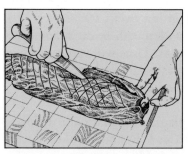

1. Cut diamond pattern lightly over the top of the fillet so the flavour of the peppercorns will permeate the meat.

BURGUNDIAN PIE

This pie can be made with a red burgundy or any type of soft red wine. The meat is cooked for some time so the flavourings mingle. It is best if it is cooked beforehand so the fat can be removed before putting the crust on top. Kaiser Fleish is a smoked bacon available at most delicatessens.

Melt the butter in a saucepan. Cut the Kaiser Fleish into small dice, removing any outside hard skin. Add to the butter and cook until the fat is transparent.

Add the shallots and minced beef and cook, giving it an occasional stir until the beef has changed colour. Add the flour and stir for a few minutes. Then add brandy and red wine and cook until it comes to the boil, stirring constantly. Add salt and pepper, bouquet garni and put a lid on the pot. Simmer gently for 30 to 45 minutes.

Meantime, melt the additional butter in a frying pan. Add the mushrooms and cook, tossing until they are just barely tender. Remove, leaving some of the butter in the pan. If the mushrooms have absorbed all of it, add a little extra.

Peel the small onions, cut them into halves or quarters and put in the pan. Season with sugar, salt and pepper and cook, tossing until they are glazed. Add the red wine and cover the pan. Cook until they are tender. They will break up a bit but this doesn't matter. Remove the onions and mix both mushroom and onion into the beef.

The crust must be put on the beef only when it is cold. Put the beef into a shallow pie dish about 30 cm (12 in) or if you use a small pie tin you can have a deeper one.

The beef should come almost to the top. Roll the puff pastry out fairly thin. Cut a strip from the pastry and place this over the edge of the dish all the way around. This makes it easier to crimp the pastry later. Then cut the remaining pastry slightly larger than the pie plate and place over the top. Crimp the edges and cut a slit in the centre.

Beat the egg with the salt and brush over the top and edges. Decorate with cut-outs if you wish. Leave to chill for about 20 minutes.

Bake in a moderately hot oven 200° C (425° F) for about 30 minutes, or until the pastry is golden and the meat heated.

INGREDIENTS

30 g (1 oz) butter
125 g (4 oz) Kaiser Fleish
1 tablespoon shallots, finely chopped
750 g (1½ lb) beef, minced
1 tablespoon flour
1 tablespoon brandy
1 cup (8 fl oz) red wine
1 teaspoon salt and pepper
bouquet garni of a stalk of celery, sprig of thyme, bay leaf, sprig of marjoram
an additional 60 g (2 oz) butter
125 g (4 oz) small, firm, button mushrooms
8 small white onions
salt and pepper
1 teaspoon sugar
1 tablespoon red wine

TO FINISH THE PIE

375 g (12 oz) puff pastry
1 egg to glaze
salt

CALVES LIVER WITH ONIONS

INGREDIENTS
500 g (1 lb) calves liver
flour for coating
30 g (1 oz) butter
1 tablespoon oil
3 white onions, very thinly sliced
3 tablespoons chicken stock
salt and pepper

This dish, if cooked well, is meltingly tender and quite delicate. Liver is a soft meat but becomes tough by overcooking. Calves liver is best served slightly pink in the centre.

Peel away any membrane left on the liver. Cut into thin slices and then cut these slices across into thin strips. Place the liver pieces in some flour. Shake away any excess by placing the strips in a sieve and shaking it.

Heat the butter and oil. Add the onions and sauté, stirring occasionally until softened and golden. Remove from the pan.

Add the liver and turn up the heat. Fry, tossing until it has changed colour. It only takes a few minutes. Return the onions, add the stock and cook. This sauce will thicken a little. Season with salt and pepper and remove from the heat.

Notes: This is very much a last minute dish, except for the onions which could be cooked during the day. Be careful not to overcook the liver, or it will spoil.

THREE STAR FILLET

INGREDIENTS
1 fillet of beef, 1.5 kg (3 lb) before
trimming
2 tablespoons oil

FILLING 1
45 g (1½ oz) butter
2 white onions, thinly sliced
1 tablespoon cream
salt and pepper

FILLING 2
60 g (2 oz) butter
250 g (8 oz) mushrooms, thinly sliced
salt and pepper
squeeze lemon juice

FILLING 3
½ bunch, 250 g (8 oz) spinach, well
washed
30 g (1 oz) butter
salt and pepper (use sparingly, anchovies
are very salty)
30 g (1 oz) gruyère cheese, grated
30 g (1 oz) anchovy fillets, mashed
1 clove garlic, crushed

TO FINISH AND ASSEMBLE
375 g (12 oz) puff pastry
1 egg
pinch salt

Place the fillet down on a board and using a piece of paper towelling to get a good grip on it, pull the skin away. Then trim the fat and the shiny part, which is a casing of tissue and sinew. Make sure that the outside of the meat is quite dry so that it will brown successfully.

Heat the oil in a frying pan, add the fillet and brown on all sides, turning constantly with 2 wooden spoons. This should only take a couple of minutes. Remove and leave aside to cool.

Cut the beef down lengthwise making three long cuts but leaving it joined at the base.

Filling 1
Melt the butter in a frying pan, add the onion and sauté, stirring occasionally until softened and very pale golden. Add the cream. Season with salt and pepper. Remove and leave to cool.

Filling 2
Melt the butter in the same pan, add the mushrooms, season with salt and pepper and fry over high heat until they are just tender. This takes only a minute. Squeeze a little lemon over them. Remove and leave to cool.

Filling 3
Remove the stalks from the spinach. Place some of the leaves together and then cut them into shreds.

Melt the butter, add spinach and toss until just becoming limp. Season with salt and pepper. Make sure it is still bright and green as it will cook even further in the fillet.

Remove, add the gruyère cheese, mashed anchovy fillets and garlic. Leave to cool.

Open up the fillet and place the onion filling on one cut, then the spinach in the centre and the mushroom in the other side.

To Assemble with Puff Pastry

Roll out the puff pastry to make a strip which is oblong and slightly longer than the fillet of beef. Place beef on one side of the pastry.

Turn up the short piece of the pastry, fold the longer piece over to meet and press together firmly. Tuck the ends under.

Beat the egg with the salt. Brush over the pastry. Roll out any little pieces to make some thin strips. Form these into a lattice over the pastry and glaze again. Prick once or twice in the centre and then place on a buttered oven tray. Chill for at least 20 minutes before cooking.

To Cook

Place in a moderately hot oven 200° C (425° F) for about 20 minutes and then remove from the oven. Leave the fillet to rest for 10 minutes in a warm place. The fillet will be rather pink; if you like it a little more well done, after cooking for 20 minutes, turn the heat down and cook another 5 minutes, then rest as above for the 10 minutes.

Notes: This dish could be done with other types of vegetables if you wish: you could use grated cooked zucchini instead of the spinach, or any vegetable you like, it is really just a matter of using your own imagination.

1. Cut three lengthwise slashes in a fillet, three-quarters way down, leaving it attached at the base.

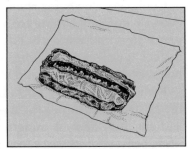

2. Insert a different filling into each slash and then place the fillet on one side of the rolled out pastry.

3. Fold the narrow strip from the end of the pastry up over the fillet and brush with beaten egg.

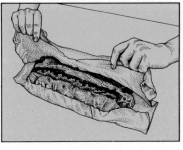

4. Then remaining pastry is folded over and pressed firmly into the egg strip so it will seal well.

LOIN OR NECK OF PORK COOKED IN MILK

INGREDIENTS
1.25 kg (2½ lb) loin or neck of pork
salt and pepper
15 g (½ oz) butter
1 tablespoon oil
2 cups (16 fl oz) milk
extra good pinch salt
a little extra pepper

This Italian dish which is very simple to prepare, uses a method of cooking which makes pork succulent and moist. The sauce tastes really good, but to our minds it doesn't look so pleasant, since the milk changes to a golden colour as it coagulates. You can serve the pork plain if you wish or spoon some of the golden curds on top.

If you are using a loin, have the butcher bone it. Remove the rind and a little of the fat. Spread the loin flat and season the inside with a little salt and pepper. Tie up firmly. The neck of pork is even nicer than the loin in this dish. However it is not easily bought from Australian butchers as they usually cut this when they prepare the shoulder. Good delicatessens or continental butchers will often sell this cut.

The fat content is spread evenly through the meat which makes it very succulent. When you buy the neck, it never has any rind attached.

Season the neck with some salt and pepper. Melt the butter and oil in a saucepan with a thick base. Add the pork and cook, turning until golden brown on all sides. Then tip out any fat or oil from the pan.

Add the milk, just a little salt and pepper (not much as during the cooking the milk reduces and it can become a bit too salty). Bring the milk to the boil and cover the pan with a lid, leaving it slightly tilted to one side to let the steam escape. Regulate the heat so it barely simmers.

Cook very slowly for about 2 hours, turning the meat about every 30 minutes, basting frequently. As it cooks the milk looks very watery and strange but disregard this. It should reduce and thicken a little, and will curdle. If this doesn't happen you can boil away some of the liquid at the finish.

Remove the piece of pork. Using a bulb baster, take some of the fat from the top of the milk. Cut the strings from the loin and cut into slices; if using a neck, place down and cut. The neck, because of its shape, carves very easily.

Serve the slices slightly overlapping.

If you wish, some of the golden milk mixture from the pan can be spooned over each slice. It tastes really delicious, even if it doesn't look attractive.

LOIN OF PORK WITH GLAZED APPLE SLICES

This loin of pork is cooked and then sliced. It is assembled with glazed apples between each slice and has a light sauce with orange shreds over the top.

Pork

Spread the pork down and season with salt and pepper. Tie with string at intervals.

Place in an ungreased baking dish. Bake for about 1½ hours or until cooked and tender. Leave in a warm place for the meat to rest before cutting.

Apples

Peel the apples carefully and core them, using a corer. Cut each apple across into about 4 slices.

Melt the butter in a frying pan. Unless you have a very large pan, you will probably need to cook the apples in several batches. Place the apples in the butter, sprinkle the top with a tiny bit of sugar. Cook until the underneath is light golden, turn and sprinkle the other side with sugar. Cook a couple of minutes. Continue until all the apple slices are done. The apples should still be firm at this stage as they will continue cooking later in the oven.

Place the apples in an ovenproof dish ready for reheating.

Sauce

Using a vegetable peeler cut thin strips from the orange. Cut these into little slivers about the width of a match. Place in a saucepan with cold water to cover them well. Cook until tender. Drain and leave aside.

Melt the butter. Add the onion and cook, stirring occasionally until softened. Add the garlic and tomato paste. Mix the cornflour with the white wine or cider and Madeira. Add to the pan with chicken stock and bring to the boil, stirring. It will be rather thin at this stage. Cook, giving an occasional stir, until it has been reduced by about a third. It should have thickened enough to coat the back of a spoon. Add the red currant jelly and orange shreds. Season if necessary.

Using a sharp knife, cut the white pith from the orange. Then loosen the segments with a knife, cutting them out so you don't have any of the membrane. Add the segments to the orange sauce and leave aside for reheating.

To Serve

Heat apples for about 12 minutes in the oven. Heat sauce.

Remove the string from the loin and cut into slices. Place a slice on a heated ovenproof platter. Place one of the apple slices on the pork, then another slice of pork, another apple slice and so on. Spoon just a little of the sauce over the top to glaze it and then return to the oven to make sure the dish is hot.

The remainder of the sauce is served with the dish.

INGREDIENTS

1.25 kg (2½ lb) loin of pork, boned and
rind removed or use 2 smaller loins
salt and pepper

APPLES
3 green apples
30 g (1 oz) butter
a little sugar

SAUCE
1 medium-sized orange
60 g (2 oz) butter
1 white onion, finely diced
small clove garlic, crushed
1 teaspoon tomato paste
1 tablespoon cornflour
½ cup (4 fl oz) dry white wine or cider
¼ cup (2 fl oz) Madeira or medium-sweet
sherry
1½ cups (12 fl oz) chicken stock
1 teaspoon red currant jelly

VEAL KIDNEYS WITH MUSTARDS

Veal kidneys are quite large and their exterior suggests a little collection of small round balls. They have quite a thick layer of fat which the butcher generally trims away. They can be cooked with the layer of fat remaining and just placed straight into the oven, as the fat makes a natural moistening.

They take about 45 minutes to cook and then the fat is just peeled away, the kidneys are sliced and served hot with some mustard. Veal kidneys, because of their delicate flavour, can also be served with various sauces.

Before cooking, check that the outside membrane has been removed from the kidneys.

Melt the butter in a frying pan. Add the whole kidneys and cook gently for about 5 minutes on each side. Remove from the pan and place in a strainer so any blood or juice which comes out will strain away.

Add the onions to the butter in the pan. There should be plenty left. Cook, giving an occasional stir until the onions are softened but don't let them go brown. Add the mustards, stock and cream. Turn the heat up very high and leave to cook until this has formed a thickish sauce.

Meantime cut the kidneys into thin slices. They will still be pink in the centre. Remove any hard centre core. When the sauce is ready, return the kidneys to the pan and cook very gently for a few minutes until heated through. Check for seasoning and serve immediately.

Kidneys spoil and toughen if overcooked or cooked over too high a heat so keep the heat gentle once you add them.

Notes: If you wish to prepare part of this dish beforehand, the kidneys could be pre-cooked in the butter and the sauce made during the day. Then add the sliced kidneys to the sauce and warm through later.

This dish can be served with a rice pilaf or squares of fried bread or toast fingers.

INGREDIENTS
3 veal kidneys
60 g (2 oz) butter
2 medium-sized white onions, finely diced
1 teaspoon French mustard
1 teaspoon dry, English-style mustard
2 teaspoons Dijon-style mustard
1 cup (8 fl oz) chicken stock
½ cup (4 fl oz) pure cream
salt and pepper

PORK AND HAM PIE

This is a dish which can be reheated successfully and is mainly served for lunch or a light informal dinner.

It is rather like some of the lovely pork mixtures which are covered with pastry and served in country restaurants in France.

Pork Filling

Melt the butter in a saucepan and add the onion. Cook, stirring, until slightly softened. Add the pork and cook, stirring until it has changed colour. Add the apple, salt and pepper and cook for about 5 minutes.

Mix the flour with the chicken stock and add to the pork. Cover the saucepan and cook for about 10 minutes. Remove this from the heat and leave to cool slightly.

Beat the eggs and fold into the cooled meat.

Ham Filling

Melt the butter in a saucepan and add the curry, fry for a minute to bring out the flavours.

Cut the ham into large dice, and add the ham to the pan and stir to coat with the curry. Remove and leave to cool.

Butter a pie dish about 23 cm (9 in) in size. Spoon half of the pork filling into the dish. Spread all the ham filling over the pork and then top with the remainder of the pork.

The filling must be cold before you cover with pastry.

Pastry Topping

Roll the puff pastry out fairly thinly. Cut a long strip and place this around the edge of the dish. This makes it easier to attach the top of the crust. Beat the egg with the salt and brush this edge with egg. From the remaining pastry cut a circle slightly larger than the pie dish. Place over the filling and tuck this under the edge of the dish. Crimp the edge neatly.

Brush the pie with egg and decorate with some cut-outs. Prick once or twice in the centre. Chill for at least 20 minutes.

To Bake

Place in a moderate oven, 200° C (425° F) for 25 to 30 minutes.

The eggs will set the filling into a nice creamy mixture.

Notes: You can vary this dish by using about 6 stoned prunes instead of or as well as the apple. Or you can use just a few soaked dried apricots, cut into small pieces.

INGREDIENTS

PORK FILLING

60 g butter (2 oz)

1 medium-sized white onion, finely diced

500 g (1 lb) pork, finely minced (not too much fat)

1 green apple, peeled and diced small

1 teaspoon salt

pepper

1 tablespoon plain flour

1 cup (8 fl oz) chicken stock

3 eggs

HAM FILLING

30 g (1 oz) butter

2 teaspoons curry powder

125 g (4 oz) ham

PASTRY TOPPING

375 g (12 oz) puff pastry

1 egg

pinch salt

A strip of puff pastry is placed around the edge of the pie dish.

VEAL LOAF WITH MUSHROOM

This is really best as a luncheon dish or at an informal dinner.

Mix the veal with the breadcrumbs, cream, egg, tomato paste, bacon, salt and pepper. Mix with your hands until smooth.

This loaf is best made in a 20 cm (8 in) sponge tin. Butter the tin. Cut out a circle of foil to fit the base and then butter this.

Place the meat into the tin and press down firmly. Using a large spoon, press down in the centre to make an indent or hollow which will be used for the filling.

Place the veal in a moderate oven, 180-190° C (350-375° F) and cook for about 20 minutes or until the meat has come away slightly from the sides. There will be quite a lot of liquid around the meat, this keeps the veal moist while it is cooking.

Remove the veal and spoon the topping into the centre hollow. Return to the oven and cook for another 15 to 20 minutes or until the topping is just firm to touch in the centre.

Topping

Melt the butter in a frying pan and add the mushrooms. Sauté over high heat until they have softened. (If the mushrooms have absorbed all the butter you may need to add a little extra.)

Add the flour and fry for a few minutes. Add milk and stir until the mixture has boiled and thickened. Remove from the heat, add the cheese, egg and egg yolk and grated rind of lemon. Mash the cream cheese and mix this into the warm mushrooms.

To Turn Out

Invert a plate over the top of the veal and turn it out. Then place another plate on top and turn over again so the topping of mushrooms is on the surface.

Notes: This dish is good hot or cold. It can also be carefully reheated. Wrap the veal in foil and reheat for about 12 minutes in a moderate oven 180-190° C (350-375° F).

INGREDIENTS
500 g (1 lb) veal, finely minced
½ cup (2 oz) breadcrumbs made from stale bread
2 tablespoons cream
1 egg
1 tablespoon tomato paste
2 rashers, 100 g (3 oz) bacon, finely diced
1 teaspoon salt
1 teaspoon pepper

TOPPING
60 g (2 oz) butter
125 g (4 oz) mushrooms
1 tablespoon plain flour
¾ cup (6 fl oz) milk
½ cup (2 oz) tasty cheese, grated
1 egg and 1 egg yolk
grated rind of 1 lemon
125 g (4 oz) cream cheese

VEAL BAKED WITH HAM AND CHEESE

This is an attractive dish when served. The meat has layers of ham and cheese which melt in the cooking and then it is carved across, so each portion of meat has the sections studded with the different flavourings.

You need to use a piece of veal which doesn't have too many muscle separations. I generally find a nice chunky, solid piece of leg veal is the best.

Place the veal in a basin or casserole. (Don't use a metal one.) Mix the brandy and sherry together and pour over the top. Turn the veal to coat.

Add to the bowl the carrot, onion, thyme, oil and a little salt

INGREDIENTS
1.5 kg (3 lb) veal
½ cup brandy
½ cup (4 fl oz) medium-sweet sherry
1 medium-sized carrot, thinly sliced
1 white onion, diced
1 sprig thyme
¼ cup (2 fl oz) olive or vegetable oil
a little salt and pepper
60 g (2 oz) butter
6 slices ham
6 slices gruyère cheese

and pepper. Cover and leave to marinate at room temperature for about 4 or 5 hours, turning the veal in the mixture. Then remove and pat dry.

Melt the butter in an ovenproof pan or casserole. Add the veal and cook, turning on all sides until it is golden.

Strain the vegetables from the marinade. Remove the veal from the pan, leave aside, add the vegetables to the butter and cook a few minutes until they are glazed. Add the marinade and bring to the boil. Remove the pan from the heat.

By this time the veal will have cooled so you can handle it. Place on a board so the flattest part is on the base. Cut slashes through almost to the base leaving it joined at the bottom. Cut about 6 deep cuts. Place 1 strip of ham and then 1 strip of cheese in each cut. Then tie with string to hold it together.

Place this piece of meat into the casserole on top of the vegetables and marinade. Place a lid on top.

It can be prepared beforehand up to this point.

To Cook

Place the casserole into a moderate oven 180-190° C (350-375° F) for about 1½ hours or until the veal is tender. You need to baste this several times during the cooking period and be sure that the casserole lid fits tightly for this dish as you need all the liquid. If it doesn't fit, place some foil over the casserole then place the lid on.

When cooked, cut away the string and keep meat warm for about 10 minutes while preparing the sauce.

Push the vegetables and liquid through a sieve. Cook for a couple of minutes in a small saucepan. Check seasoning.

Serve a little of this over the veal. Carve the veal across the ham rather than down the same way you originally cut the meat.

1. Cut about six thick slashes, three-quarters way through browned section of veal, leaving it joined at the base.

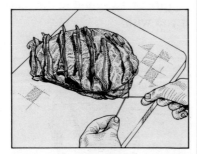

2. Place strip of ham, then cheese in each cut and tie with string to hold the slices together.

LOIN OF PORK WITH GREEN PEPPERCORNS, PRUNES AND HAZELNUTS

INGREDIENTS

1.25 kg (2½ lb) loin of pork, boned and
  with rind removed or 2 smaller loins
salt
1 cup weak black tea
12 prunes
1 tablespoon green peppercorns
2 tablespoons hazelnuts, very finely
  chopped
1 bare teaspoon salt
1 teaspoon curry powder

SAUCE

½ cup (4 fl oz) chicken stock
½ cup (4 fl oz) thick or pure cream

The prunes and nuts make this quite a rich dish so small servings are ample.

Place the pork on a board, spread out and sprinkle the inside of the loin lightly with salt.

Heat the tea and pour over the prunes. Leave to stand for about 10 minutes and then drain. Be sure to remove the stones from the prunes.

Crush the green peppercorns with the flat part of a knife and spread a thin layer over the pork. Then sprinkle hazelnuts over this. Arrange a layer of prunes down the centre of the loin. Roll up and tie securely at intervals with string, making a nice firm roll of meat. Place in baking tin.

Mix the salt and curry powder together. Rub over the outside of the meat.

Bake in a moderate oven 180-190° C (350-375° F) for approximately 1½ hours or until cooked. There is no need to baste the meat or turn it.

Remove from the tin and tip out all the fat.

Sauce

Add the stock and cream to the tin. Place over heat and cook, stirring to get up all the nice little brown bits that will be on the base. Leave to cook for a few minutes until it has thickened. Pour through a strainer and serve with the pork.

Notes: This dish is also delicious cold and looks most attractive with the studded centre of prunes and nuts.

When you chop the nuts they must be rather fine or the texture isn't so good in the centre. You can use ground hazelnuts if you wish.

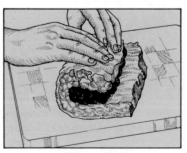

1. Roll the pork over firmly. The two edges of the loin should meet.

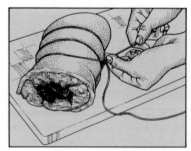

2. Form into a good firm roll and tie securely at intervals with string.

Tagliatelle with Sautéed Vegetables (page 116)

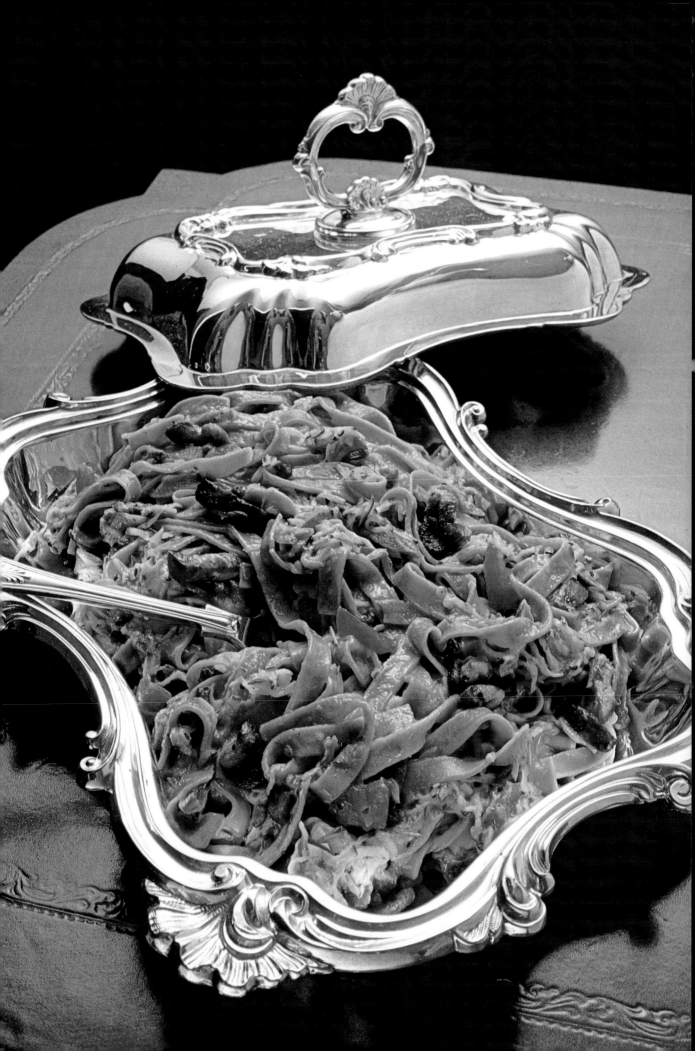

FISH

Fish is very much an untapped area in Australia and although we have a natural abundance, the choice of fish sold in shops is very limited. To add to the confusion, fish varieties in one state change their names in another.

As this isn't a specialised fish book, I have chosen just a few dishes which have a method of cooking suitable for many varieties of fish.

When you buy fish it should always have a fresh odour and the eyes must be protruding, bright and clear. The scales should have a sheen and the flesh must be slightly elastic. Fish loses flavour more rapidly when frozen and is never as juicy. If you can, go to the markets or to a reliable fish shop where you may be able to buy fresh fish.

The main rule with fish is never to overcook it. Fish takes much less time to cook than meat and does not rely on weight so much as thickness. A thick cut of fish needs more time per kilogram than a thin fish with exactly the same weight. When it is cooked, fish should be opaque and lift away from the bone.

FISH WITH WHITE WINE AND TARRAGON SAUCE

I have prepared this dish with various types of fish: John Dory, fillets of snapper, the choice is yours. But don't use frozen fish, and finely textured, thin fish such as whiting are not so suitable.

Spread the fillets of fish out on a board. Be sure there are no little bits of fin or bone left. Mix the lemon juice and Worcestershire sauce together. Brush this over the fish and leave to stand for about 10 minutes.

Heat the butter in a large frying pan. When foaming add the fish and cook gently on both sides. Timing will depend on the type of fish used but do not overcook as it will continue cooking while you make the sauce. Remove the fish to a warmed platter and cover with some foil.

Add the shallots and white wine to the same pan. Have the heat high and cook rapidly for a couple of minutes. Add the pure cream and tarragon and cook until thick and golden in colour. In a shallow pan this will not take long. Add parsley, salt and pepper.

Return the fish to the pan, spooning a little of the sauce over the top and then serve immediately.

INGREDIENTS
500 g (1 lb) fish fillets
juice of 1 lemon
2 teaspoons Worcestershire sauce
60 g (2 oz) butter
1 tablespoon shallots, finely chopped
½ cup (4 fl oz) dry white wine
¾ cup (6 fl oz) pure cream
pinch dried or 1 teaspoon fresh tarragon
1 tablespoon parsley, finely chopped
salt and pepper

Whiting with Orange Sauce (page 94)

FILLETS OF FISH WITH ONIONS

6 fillets of fish
salt and pepper
45 g (1½ oz) butter
1 tablespoon vegetable oil
3 medium-sized white onions, thinly sliced
2 tablespoons dry white wine
a little salt and pepper

TOPPING

30 g (1 oz) butter
½ cup (2 oz) breadcrumbs made from stale bread
1 tablespoon parsley
rind of 1 lemon, grated

Any boneless fillets of fish can be used for this dish. It must be fresh fish. Whiting is particularly good served this way.

Check that no bones remain in the fish, season the fillets with salt and pepper and leave aside.

Melt the butter with the oil in a frying pan. Add the onions and sauté, stirring occasionally until they are quite limp and soft and have just started to become pale gold in colour.

Remove from the heat and add the white wine to the onions. Season with a little salt and pepper and place them in a shallow ovenproof dish. The size of the dish used depends on the size of the fish. There isn't any need to grease the dish as the onions will be buttery enough. Place the fish in one layer on top of the onions. Make sure that when you put the fish on top the fillets are close together, this will keep them moist.

Topping

Melt the butter and add the crumbs. Toss until the crumbs are slightly golden. Remove from the heat and mix with parsley and lemon rind. Spread this over the top of the fish. Place into a moderate oven 180-190° C (350-375° F) for 12 to 15 minutes, or until the fish fillets are tender. The timing depends on the type of fish used. Serve some of the onions underneath each fillet.

WHITING WITH ORANGE SAUCE

INGREDIENTS

6 fillets of whiting
salt and pepper

STUFFING

60 g (2 oz) butter
⅓ cup (2 oz) celery, finely diced
1 small white onion, finely chopped
¾ cup (3 oz) breadcrumbs made from stale bread
rind of 1 orange, grated
salt and pepper

SAUCE

2 teaspoons sugar
¼ teaspoon ginger
1 teaspoon dry, English-style mustard
2 teaspoons cornflour
grated rind of 1 large orange
1 cup orange juice
1 tablespoon lemon juice
segments from 2 oranges

Whiting has a particularly light flavour which is excellent with orange. If you want to substitute another type of fish you must use a finely textured fish and to do the dish successfully, it must be boned out. In this dish, the whiting has a stuffing flavoured with orange and then is cooked in the sauce. It is excellent as a first course. To serve it as a main dish, double the quantity.

Trim any little pieces of fin from the whiting and place the fillets down on a board. Remove the few bones from the end by cutting a slit. Then push the ends together. Season with salt and pepper. Place the fillets so that the dark skin is towards you and the white part underneath.

Stuffing

Melt the butter in a small frying pan. Add the celery and onion and sauté, stirring occasionally until soft but not coloured.

Place the breadcrumbs in a bowl, add the orange rind and mix the onion and celery into this. Season.

Take a little of this stuffing and place some on half of each whiting fillet. Fold each fillet over and press down gently. They will cook flat and the stuffing will remain in.

Place the whiting in a buttered shallow ovenproof dish. Make sure the dish is small so they just fit snugly, otherwise the sauce tends to cook away. Place them alternately with the thick end on one side, thin the other.

Sauce

Mix the sugar, ginger, mustard and cornflour together with the orange rind, juice, lemon juice. Place in a small saucepan and heat until it comes to the boil. Remove and pour over the whiting. Then place some foil over the top of the dish and tuck it well down so that it will keep all the moisture in.

Bake in a moderate oven, 180-190° C (350-375° F) for about 15 or 20 minutes until the fish is cooked. Test the thickest part with the point of a knife. Don't overcook this fish as it is nicest when just done.

Remove the skin from the orange and cut out segments. Add the segments to the top of the whiting and return to the oven for about a minute just to heat them through.

Serve the whiting with some of the sauce over the top and a couple of orange segments.

Notes: When you make the orange sauce, taste it as oranges vary considerably at different times of the year. It should be just slightly tart. You can adjust if it is too sweet by adding a little lemon juice, or if too sour, by adding a little extra sugar.

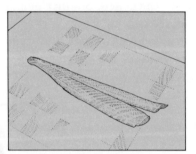

1. Remove top fin and small section of bone from fillet by making a "V" cut.

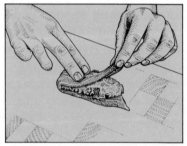

2. Place a portion of stuffing on half the fillet. Fold over and press down.

3. Place in an ovenproof dish so they fit closely together.

4. Cut segments out from the orange, leaving the membrane behind.

SCALLOPS IN OYSTER SAUCE

The scallops are cooked first and then mixed with the oyster sauce. The oysters are actually sieved or puréed to give a smooth mixture. It's an incredibly good combination, although rather a luxury dish.

Remove the coral from the scallops. Keep separate. Bring the wine, water and salt to the boil. Add the white part of the scallops. Turn off the heat. Leave to sit for 2 minutes, add the coral and leave another minute. As the scallops will be cooked again with the sauce this is quite sufficient time. Drain, but keep the liquid.

INGREDIENTS
500 g (1 lb) scallops
½ cup (4 fl oz) water
½ cup (4 fl oz) dry white wine
½ teaspoon salt

MUSHROOM MIXTURE
60 g (2 oz) butter
125 g (4 oz) mushrooms, thinly sliced
salt and pepper
squeeze of lemon juice

Mushroom Mixture
Melt the butter in a frying pan, add the mushrooms, season with salt, pepper and the squeeze of lemon juice and cook over high heat for a couple of minutes or until they are tender. Remove and mix with the scallops.

SAUCE
30 g (1 oz) butter
1 tablespoon flour
1 cup (8 fl oz) liquid from the scallops
1 dozen oysters
2 tablespoons cream

Sauce
Melt the butter in a small saucepan and add the flour. Cook, stirring until the flour is slightly granulated. Add the liquid from the scallops and stir constantly until thickened. Simmer gently for a couple of minutes. Add the oysters and cream and cook another minute. Oysters only take a moment to cook and some of the flavour is lost if you simmer them for too long.

Push this sauce through a moulin or blend it. Check for seasoning and add if necessary.

Mix the sauce gently into the scallops and mushrooms. Place in either individual small dishes, scallop shells or one large dish.

TOPPING
2 ripe tomatoes, peeled
salt and pepper
a little sugar
3 tablespoons breadcrumbs made from stale bread
2 tablespoons parmesan cheese, finely grated
30 g (1 oz) butter, cut into small pieces

Topping
Cut the tomatoes into thin slices. Arrange these over the scallops. In small individual dishes, usually two overlapping slices is sufficient. Season with salt, pepper and a tiny bit of sugar and then sprinkle with breadcrumbs and cheese. Dot the butter over the top. Place in the oven to heat until bubbling at the edges.

Notes: This dish reheats most successfully and you can prepare it about 6 hours beforehand and keep refrigerated. Don't overcook or the scallops toughen. If you are using small dishes, bake for perhaps 10 to 12 minutes in a moderate oven, 180-190° C (350-375° F). For a large casserole, about 15 to 20 minutes.

PRAWNS WITH ALMOND CRUMBS

This dish really needs to be made with raw or green prawns. These can usually be bought at good fish shops or the markets and even if they have been frozen the dish is quite successful. Because they are flattened out, two prawns look quite a reasonable serve on a plate.

It is a little hard to calculate the exact quantity of crumbs, but this recipe does approximately 750 g (1½ lbs) raw prawns.

Peel the prawns but leave the little tail piece on. Split the prawns down the centre to open them out, remove vein. Flatten very gently to make a round shape.

Mix together the milk, salt and curry powder in a shallow dish. Add the prawns to this milk mixture and let stand for 1 hour. Remove and place on kitchen paper to drain.

Dip each prawn in a little plain flour and shake away the excess. Then dip in egg.

Mix the crumbs, almonds and pepper together and dip the prawns into this, pressing the crumbs down firmly. Place them in the refrigerator for a short time to firm up the crumbs.

To Cook

You need a large frying pan, or cook the prawns in two batches.

Melt the butter and oil together and when foaming add the prawns. They only take a minute or so on each side. The prawns are nicest served as soon as they are cooked.

You can serve with some lemon on the side or with the Chutney Cream.

Chutney Cream

Chop any little pieces in the mango chutney. Mix with the cream, curry and salt. Leave aside.

Heat the oil in a small saucepan and add the apple and tomato. Fry, stirring for a couple of minutes and then place a lid on the pan. Cook covered until quite tender. Push this through a sieve, pressing down hard to get all the juices out. Cool, then add to the mango cream mixture. Chutney Cream can be kept refrigerated for several days.

Notes: This dish goes well with a cucumber salad, served crisp and cold. The contrast between the hot prawns and cold cucumber is really good. This dish can't be cooked and reheated as prawns become tough and hard with a second cooking.

INGREDIENTS

750 g (1½ lbs) prawns in the shell
1 cup (8 fl oz) milk
½ teaspoon salt
1 teaspoon curry powder
flour
2 eggs
¾ cup (3 oz) breadcrumbs made from stale bread
¾ cup (5 oz) almonds, finely ground
a little white pepper

TO COOK

60 g (2 oz) butter
4 tablespoons oil

CHUTNEY CREAM

1 tablespoon mango chutney
1 tablespoon cream, lightly whipped
1 teaspoon curry powder
pinch salt
1 tablespoon oil
1 medium-sized apple, peeled and diced small
1 small ripe tomato, peeled, some seeds removed and cut in tiny pieces

PRAWNS BAKED WITH FETA

INGREDIENTS

*500 g (1 lb) prawns, use green, raw prawns
  if possible*
2 tablespoons olive oil
60 g (2 oz) black olives
1 clove garlic, crushed
pepper, no salt
125 g (4 oz) feta cheese

TOMATO SAUCE

500 g (1 lb) ripe tomatoes, peeled
1 tablespoon olive oil
*a little salt, (use sparingly, fetta cheese can
  be salty)*
pepper
pinch sugar

This is a bright and colourful dish with all the lovely aroma and flavours of the Greek Isles. Feta cheese can be bought in most good quality delicatessens and is usually kept in a container of brine. Feta varies from mild to very salty. If you taste and find it is a little too salty, cover the cheese with some milk for about 20 minutes to reduce this. Drain and then use.

Prawns
Remove the shells from the prawns but leave the tail piece on. Put the olive oil in a frying pan, add the prawns and cook until they have just changed colour on the outside, turning them once.

Stone the olives and add to the pan with the prawns, stirring to coat them with oil. Add the tomato sauce, garlic and pepper and cook for half a minute, mixing the prawns gently so they are coated with the sauce. Transfer to a shallow casserole.

Cut the feta cheese into small pieces. Scatter these evenly over the top of the dish. This part can be prepared beforehand and then reheated.

Bake in a moderate oven until heated through and the cheese has become soft.

Tomato Sauce
Cut the tomatoes into small pieces. Place a saucepan with the oil, salt, pepper and sugar and cook, stirring until the mixture forms a thick sauce. This takes about 15 to 20 minutes.

Notes: Don't overcook or the prawns will toughen. Feta cheese seems to vary, some melts more than others on top of the dish but this doesn't make much difference to the finished flavour.

The flavour of the olive oil isn't strong but it does seem to bring out the other flavours of the olives, prawns, garlic and tomatoes. However if you prefer lighter vegetable oils for cooking you can use these.

SCALLOPS WITH GREEN PEPPERCORN SAUCE

INGREDIENTS

500 g (1 lb) scallops
½ cup (4 fl oz) dry white wine
½ cup (4 fl oz) water
½ teaspoon salt
½ cup (4 fl oz) pure cream
3 teaspoons green peppercorns
1 medium-sized carrot
*125 g (4 oz) small white button
  mushrooms*

This dish can be cooked rapidly once you have cleaned the scallops. The amount of green peppercorns makes it medium hot; you can adjust as you wish. If you can't get green peppercorns, use a little white pepper but don't use black peppercorns.

The peppercorns you have left can be kept refrigerated in a small container in their brine, or else we find it best to freeze them in a wrapping of plastic wrap and foil. They will thaw in a couple of minutes. Never use the brine which comes around these as it is too hot and strong.

Clean the scallops, keep white part and coral separate. Heat the white wine, water and salt in a small saucepan. Add the scallops when the wine is boiling, adding the white part first. Turn the heat off stand for about 2 minutes, then add the coral and leave for 1 minute. Drain but keep the liquid. Cover the scallops to keep them moist.

Place this liquid in a frying pan with the cream and boil rapidly until it has been reduced to about half. Add the peppercorns and continue cooking until the sauce is thickened and pale golden. Add the scallops and warm through, mixing with the sauce. Check seasoning.

Preparation of Carrot and Mushrooms

Peel or scrape the carrot and cut into three sections. Then cut these sections into halves and into small matchstick pieces.

Place these in a small saucepan with some water and salt and cook until just tender. Because they are so small they will only take a few minutes. Drain and leave aside.

Remove stalks from the mushrooms and cut into thin slices.

When the scallop dish is cooked and the scallops have been warmed, add the carrot and mushrooms. Leave to cook very gently for another couple of minutes. This will be sufficient time to cook the mushrooms and heat the carrot. Because the scallops are barely cooked in the beginning they won't toughen.

Notes: This can be served plain or with some small pastry cut-outs or a little rice. There should be just enough sauce to keep everything moist and it will be very light in flavour because no flour has been used.

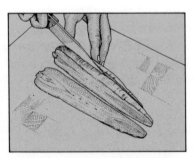

1. Cut the carrot into three lengthwise.

2. Cut in half across.

3. Cut into matchstick pieces.

SCALLOPS NASSIKAS

INGREDIENTS

ZUCCHINI MIXTURE
500 g (1 lb) zucchini
1 teaspoon salt
60 g (2 oz) butter
a little white pepper

SCALLOPS
500 g (1 lb) scallops
½ cup (4 fl oz) water
¾ cup (6 fl oz) dry champagne
¼ teaspoon salt

SAUCE
45 g (1½ oz) butter
1 medium-sized white onion, finely diced
1 teaspoon curry powder
1 tablespoon flour
liquid from the scallops
½ cup (4 fl oz) cream

TOPPING
⅓ cup (1 oz) breadcrumbs made from stale bread

Jim Nassikas is the president of Stanford Court Hotel in San Francisco, a comparatively new hotel which, in the short time it has been built, has earned international recognition as well as winning every major American hotel award. Not one of the largest hotels, it has a warmth and personal service which is becoming rare in the world of chain-operated, mass-produced accommodation. A completely dedicated and untiring hotelier, Jim Nassikas was the inspiration in the creation of the Stanford Court Hotel and this dish has been named in his honour.

Zucchini Mixture
Discard the ends of the zucchini and grate the vegetable on a coarse grater into a large bowl. Add the salt either in several layers or sprinkle over the top and then stir with a fork to mix through. Stand at room temperature for 1 hour. At the end of this time there will be quite a lot of liquid in the bowl. Take out the zucchini in handfuls and press firmly to squeeze out the liquid, just pushing it through a sieve is not adequate. Place the zucchini on some kitchen paper to completely dry it.

Melt the butter in a frying pan. Add the zucchini and stir with a fork as it tends to pack into a mass after you have squeezed it. Season with a little pepper. Cook until just barely softened, this only takes about 4 minutes. It will continue cooking for a moment when you remove it so don't overcook. Remove to a bowl and leave aside.

Scallops
Remove the coral from the scallops and clean them. Heat the water, champagne and salt in a saucepan and when boiling add the scallops. Turn the heat off, leave 2 minutes, add the coral and then leave another minute. Drain the scallops but keep the liquid for the sauce. Cover to keep them moist.

Sauce
Melt the butter and add the onion. Sauté, stirring occasionally until softened. Add the curry powder and fry for a moment to bring out the flavours. Add the flour and fry, stirring a little longer. Add all the liquid from the scallops and stir until it comes to the boil and has thickened. Then add the cream and leave to cook gently until the sauce coats the back of a spoon. This will take at least 30 to 45 minutes and by gently cooking the sauce it will have much more flavour.

To Assemble
Place a layer of scallops in a buttered shallow dish, or use individual dishes. Spread a layer of zucchini over the top of the scallops. Coat this with the sauce.

To Finish
Place the breadcrumbs on a scone tray or baking sheet and place in the oven until they are pale gold in colour. Sprinkle these over the sauce.

Heat this in a moderate oven 180-190° C (350-375° F) until heated through and the edges are bubbling. Do not overcook.

Notes: Some of the various stages of this dish can be prepared beforehand although it is nicest if assembled near to serving time. You can cook the zucchini and leave it refrigerated, cook the scallops and then leave them, but be sure to add a few spoonfuls of their liquid so they will stay moist.

The sauce can also be prepared during the day and then gently warmed before pouring over the zucchini. When this is served a small amount of liquid forms under the zucchini and over the scallops since even though it is drained well zucchini always gives out a small amount of water.

If you don't want to use champagne a dry white wine could be used as an alternative.

COLD SCALLOPS IN CITRUS SAUCE

Scallops are generally served hot, but on a warm day a dish of these iced scallops in the light orange and lemon sauce is most refreshing. The dish improves by being made about 12 hours before eating.

Separate the coral from the scallops. Heat the water and wine with the salt in a small saucepan. When the water is boiling, add the scallops, turn off the heat and leave 2 minutes. Add the coral and leave another minute and then drain. Unless they are really large scallops they will be sufficiently cooked.

Citrus Sauce
Mix in a bowl the lemon and orange juices, the cayenne, salt and castor sugar with the orange-flavoured liqueur. Add the scallops, cover and keep refrigerated, giving them an occasional stir.

To Finish
Add the spring onions and parsley to the scallops.

Remove the rind from the orange, being careful to take away most of the white pith. Then using a small sharp knife cut out the segments, leaving behind the membranes between each one. Add these segments to the scallops.

If you have the patience, the sultana grapes are nicer peeled. This is rather tedious but worth the trouble. Either way, add them last and mix the ingredients together.

Serve with some bread and butter or crusty bread.

Notes: Because this dish has a lot of juice you need to serve the scallops in either small shells or baby soufflé dishes. You can't put them on a flat plate or the juices spread out and they don't look nearly so attractive.

INGREDIENTS
500 g (1 lb) scallops
½ cup (4 fl oz) water
½ cup (4 fl oz) dry white wine
½ teaspoon salt

CITRUS SAUCE
⅓ cup (3 fl oz) lemon juice
⅓ cup (3 fl oz) orange juice
pinch cayenne pepper
a little salt
1 teaspoon castor sugar
1 tablespoon orange-flavoured liqueur

TO FINISH
⅓ cup (2 oz) spring onions, cut into chunky pieces
3 tablespoons parsley, finely chopped
segments from 2 medium-sized oranges
125 g (4 oz) green sultana grapes

Vegetables can make the most interesting of all dishes and all they require is a little tender loving care. One beautifully cooked vegetable is worth three indifferent ones and yet there is a strange feeling which is particularly strong in restaurants that unless the plate is completely covered, the meal has been inadequate. The easiest way to cover the plate is with a variety of vegetables, but it is just not possible to cook many and do them all successfully.

You should also give some thought to the compatibility of the flavour of the vegetable you are serving with the flavour of the meats they are to accompany.

Many of these dishes can be served as a separate course after the meat. If you do this then do not serve a salad.

BEAN AND PEA PURÉE

INGREDIENTS

1 kg (2 lb) green beans, cut into short pieces
500 g (1 lb) peas
salt
little sugar
little mint
60 g (2 oz) butter
1 large white onion, finely diced
2 tablespoons thick or pure cream

On their own, beans don't make a good purée as they tend to become rather watery. You can always purée them with potato but they are really too delicate for this. When combined with peas, the peas give additional flavour and colour, as well as thickening the purée.

It is good with almost any meat, particularly lamb, and has an advantage in that it can be prepared beforehand, even the day before, and then reheated.

Although the quantities may look large you lose a certain amount by this method of cooking.

Cook the beans in a pot of salted water until they are quite tender. For this dish the vegetables must be well cooked as firm beans are very difficult to purée. Drain and run cold water over them until they are cool so they will keep a good colour.

Cook the peas in a pot of water, with salt, a little sugar and some mint until quite tender. Drain these also, and run cold water over them.

Melt the butter in a saucepan or large frying pan. Add the onion and sauté, stirring occasionally until softened. Then add the beans and peas to the pan and stir to coat with butter.

Remove and either push through a moulin, blend or purée the mixture. A food processor can be used, this does not make it as smooth but it does not really matter.

Reheat the vegetables, adding the cream. Taste for seasoning. The purée should just hold a shape when you mound it but not be stiff. If you find it too wet, you can cook it in a pan to dry it.

Notes: Some of the round firm, stringless beans are rather hard to purée. If you can buy only these, cut them into small pieces before cooking.

If you use beans with strings and are going to use a moulin, there isn't any need to string them. However if you are using a food processor to finish the purée, it is better to string the beans.

CAULIFLOWER

The heart of the cauliflower should be firm and white and surrounded by bright green leaves. If it is shading to cream or brown and the leaves have started to yellow, it is too old.

When the cauliflower has been kept for some time, it will have a strong odour and flavour when cooked.

It cooks more evenly if the little flowerettes are divided and the stem is cut into slices.

CAULIFLOWER IN ANCHOVY SAUCE

A dish which has rather pungent flavourings and so is good with steak or on its own as a side dish.

Cut the centre stalk from the cauliflower. This is not used in the dish, but you can keep it aside and later add to a soup.

Break the cauliflower into small flowerettes. Bring the pot of salted water to the boil and add the cauliflower. Cook until just barely tender and then drain. Run cold water over them to refresh and prevent further cooking. Drain the flowerettes and place on kitchen paper to dry. If any moisture remains in them the dish becomes watery.

Sauce

Melt the butter in a small saucepan and add the onion. Sauté, stirring occasionally until softened. Cut the tomatoes into small pieces. Add to the onion and cook without a lid until you have a thick mixture. This usually takes about 25 to 30 minutes. Add the pepper and anchovies. Don't add salt as the anchovies supply this. Add sugar if sauce is too sharp.

Warm a small pudding basin by filling with boiling water. Tip out the water and wipe it dry. Mix the cauliflower into the tomato sauce and stir gently to coat it. Cook for a few minutes to warm the cauliflower through.

Turn the cauliflower into the basin and press down gently with the back of a spoon. Upend the basin onto a dinner plate and it will unmould easily. Sprinkle the top with the parsley. Once you start to serve this then the mould breaks up but it makes an attractive presentation.

INGREDIENTS
½ large or 1 small cauliflower
a large pot of salted water

SAUCE
45 g (1½ oz) butter
1 medium-sized white onion, finely chopped
375 g (12 oz) ripe tomatoes, peeled
a little black pepper
½ tin 30 g (1 oz) anchovies
½ teaspoon sugar (if needed)
1 tablespoon parsley, finely chopped

CUCUMBERS

Cucumbers are very popular for salads but not often served as a hot vegetable and yet they make an interesting change. Because of the amount of natural water it is best to boil them for only a few minutes before using as a vegetable dish. When serving cold, cucumber should always be salted to accentuate the flavour and remove the water content. If you have a cucumber which is bitter, this preliminary salting will draw out any bitterness.

When you buy cucumbers, the skin should always be bright green and the ends firm. A cucumber which has a soft end or any withered skin will be coarse.

CUCUMBERS AND MUSHROOM MEDLEY

INGREDIENTS
2 medium-sized cucumbers
1 cup (8 fl oz) chicken stock
45 g (1½ oz) butter
1 tablespoon flour
1 teaspoon curry powder
125 g (4 oz) small button mushrooms, fresh
¼ cup (2 fl oz) cream
1 tablespoon parsley, finely chopped
salt and pepper

Peel the cucumber and cut into halves lengthwise. Remove seeds. Cut in slices about 1 cm (½ in) thick. Place in a saucepan and add the chicken stock. Bring to the boil and cook for about 3 minutes. Drain and keep the stock.

Melt the butter in the same saucepan. Add the flour and curry powder and leave to fry for a few minutes, stirring until the flour is slightly granulated but don't let it brown. Add the chicken stock from the cucumber and, stirring constantly, bring to the boil.

Add the cucumbers, small whole mushrooms and simmer uncovered until the cucumber is just barely cooked. This usually takes between 5 and 8 minutes. Add cream and check seasoning, sprinkle parsley over the top and mix in.

This sauce is on the thin side. It's meant to be like this. If you would prefer a thick sauce, after bringing to the boil, and before adding the cucumber and mushroom, leave the sauce to cook without a lid until it has become fairly thick.

GLAZED CARROTS AND ONIONS

INGREDIENTS
1 bunch baby carrots
3 medium-sized white onions
60 g (2 oz) butter
salt and pepper
1 teaspoon sugar
2 tablespoons chicken stock
a little parsley, finely chopped

Scrape or peel the carrots and remove the ends. Peel the onions and cut them into quarters. Separate the onions so you have lots of little separate sections.

Melt the butter in a small pan and add the carrots and onions. Season with salt, pepper and sugar and cook for about 10 minutes or until lightly golden and glazed on the outside.

Add the chicken stock, place a lid on the pot and cook gently, shaking the pan occasionally, until they are tender. If there is too much liquid left, remove the lid, turn up the heat and cook rapidly until the liquid has all evaporated.

Sprinkle with some parsley and serve.

Notes: This can be prepared beforehand and then reheated.

CAULIFLOWER SAUTÉ

A dish of slightly crispy cauliflower which is really tasty enough to be a first course in itself.

Remove the tough centre core from the cauliflower. Cut the stalk away and cut this into slices. Cut the flowerettes up small.

Bring the pot of water to the boil and add the cauliflower. Cook only for a few minutes, so that it is still crisp. Drain. Run cold water through the vegetable so it won't continue cooking. Place on kitchen paper to drain it well.

Melt the butter in a frying pan. Add the pine kernels. Cook a minute to coat them with the butter. Add the garlic and cauliflower pieces and a little black pepper and salt if needed. Toss until the cauliflower is hot and the pine kernels golden. Add parsley, toss and serve immediately.

Notes: You can prepare the cauliflower beforehand by pre-cooking, but only toss with the pine kernels and butter at the last moment before serving.

INGREDIENTS
½ large or 1 small cauliflower
large pot of salted water
60 g (2 oz) butter
2 tablespoons pine kernels
1 clove garlic, crushed
black pepper
a little salt if needed
1 tablespoon parsley, finely chopped

TURNIPS

Unfortunately most of the turnips in the shops tend to be far too large. If you can, try to buy small to medium-sized ones. When they are smaller they are much more delicate in texture and flavour. A turnip should be smooth and hard to the touch, have bright green tops and only just a couple of fibrous roots at the end. Never buy any that look soft or wrinkled or have limp yellowing leaves.

They can be a delicious vegetable and if blanched first, most of the strong flavour will disappear. They can then be cooked in butter and become quite rich and sweet.

GLAZED TURNIPS

Peel the turnips. Cut them into wedges, like an apple. Place them in a saucepan with some cold water. Add a little salt and bring to the boil. Drain. Melt the butter and add the turnip wedges. Season with salt, pepper and the sugar. Cook, shaking or stirring the pan over fairly high heat until they are glazed. They will still be firm at this stage.

Add the stock or water and place a lid on the saucepan. Cook turnips over low heat, shaking the pan occasionally, until they are quite tender. If there is any liquid left around them, turn up the heat and boil them rapidly for a few minutes until the liquid has evaporated and formed a glaze.

Timing for the cooking depends on the size and age of the turnips being used.

INGREDIENTS
6 medium-sized or 12 small turnips
30 g (1 oz) butter
salt and pepper
1 teaspoon sugar
1 tablespoon chicken stock (or water)

EGGPLANT AUBERGINE

Although you can buy this vegetable all year round in Australia, it is still not greatly used in cooking and yet there are dozens of interesting and different methods of cooking it.

The skin should be shiny and the eggplant firm. Don't buy it if it is wrinkled and dull as it will be unpleasant in flavour. When eggplant is fresh the seeds are small but if it is stored, the seeds mature and become larger and the flesh bitter. This bitterness can be reduced by sprinkling the flesh with salt and leaving to stand. The liquid will work its way out. The flesh is then wiped or washed and the eggplant dried on kitchen paper. This also has the added advantage of reducing the water content of the vegetable. Salting does improve the flavour considerably.

BAKED EGGPLANT WITH SAVOURY TOPPING

INGREDIENTS

500 g (1 lb) medium-sized or small
eggplants
salt
flour
some oil
1 clove garlic, crushed
1 tablespoon tomato paste

TOPPING

15 g (½ oz) butter
3 tablespoons pine kernels
3 tablespoons tasty cheese, finely grated
4 tablespoons breadcrumbs
salt and pepper

The eggplant is sliced and then cooked in oil and the topping added. After this it is baked. It looks most attractive but because of the rather pungent flavourings and slight oiliness of the eggplant it is best served with meats which are not fatty. Goes well with steak, veal or chicken.

Discard the stalk end from the eggplant and cut the vegetable into slices lengthwise. Don't make them too thin, they should be at least 2 cm (¾ in) thick.

Place them on a board and sprinkle with salt. Leave to stand for about 30 minutes or even longer. The eggplant will weep and the salt draws out any bitterness. Pat the slices dry.

Place some flour on a piece of greaseproof paper. Place the eggplant onto this and coat lightly. Dust away any excess flour. Heat enough oil to cover the base of a frying pan. As eggplant tends to absorb oil you probably need to add more as it cooks. Cook over fairly high heat until slices are golden on both sides and just barely soft. Place them on some kitchen paper and leave them to drain. Generally you need to do the eggplant in several batches as it takes up quite a lot of room in a pan.

When they are all done they can be put on the tray ready for the baking but must be in one layer.

Mix the garlic and tomato paste together and spread a little of this over the eggplant.

Topping
Melt the butter in a frying pan. Add the pine kernels and toss for a couple of minutes until they are pale golden. Remove. Mix the tasty cheese, breadcrumbs and a little salt and pepper with the pine kernels. Spread a thin layer of this over the eggplant.

Bake in a moderate oven 180-190° C (350-375° F) for about 12 minutes or until the topping is golden.

Note: This dish can be completely prepared beforehand and then baked later.

GRATIN OF EGGPLANT

A very light eggplant dish where the vegetable is covered with eggs and cream and then baked. Finally it is topped with a fresh tomato sauce. It reheats most successfully, even a day after it is first cooked.

Peel the eggplants and cut into slices, lengthwise if they are small eggplants, across if large. Place down on a board and sprinkle with salt. Leave to stand for 30 minutes or even longer. The eggplant will weep and this draws out the bitter juices. Drain, and pat the slices dry. Dust them lightly with flour, shake away any excess.

Heat enough oil to film the base of a frying pan and cook egg-plant on both sides over fairly high heat until golden and just cooked through. Remove and place on paper towelling to drain. Usually you need to keep adding a little extra oil to the pan and do them in several batches.

Lightly oil a shallow gratin dish. I use one about 23 cm (9 in) x 15 cm (6 in). Place the eggplant in the dish and have the slices overlapping.

Beat the eggs with cream, season. Pour this over the eggplant and bake in a moderate oven 180-190° C (350-375° F) until it is just set. It usually takes about 20 to 25 minutes.

Sauce

Melt the butter in a small saucepan. Add the onion and cook, stirring occasionally until slightly golden, but do not let it brown. Add the tomato, salt, pepper and sugar. Cook gently until the mixture is thickened and then sieve.

Pour the sauce over the top of the eggplant.

Topping

Mix the crumbs and cheese together. Sprinkle the topping over the tomatoes and return the dish to the oven for another 5 minutes to heat the tomato sauce and melt the cheese.

Note: If you wish, instead of putting the dish back in the oven you can grill the top for a couple of minutes.

INGREDIENTS
500 g (1 lb) eggplant
salt
a little plain flour
some oil
2 eggs
½ cup (4 fl oz) cream

TOMATO SAUCE
30 g (1 oz) butter
1 small white onion, finely diced
350 g (12 oz) tomatoes, unpeeled, roughly chopped
salt and pepper
¼ teaspoon sugar

TOPPING
3 tablespoons breadcrumbs made from stale bread
2 tablespoons parmesan cheese, finely grated

1. The eggplant slices are arranged in a shallow ovenproof dish with the slices slightly overlapping.

2. A mixture of egg and cream is poured over the top before placing the dish in the oven.

'GRITTI' STUFFED ZUCCHINI

INGREDIENTS
6 medium-sized zucchini
60 g (2 oz) butter
2 medium-sized white onions, finely diced

BÉCHAMEL SAUCE
30 g (1 oz) butter
2 teaspoons plain flour
½ cup (4 fl oz) milk
salt and pepper
a pinch mustard

REMAINING INGREDIENTS
*½ cup (2 oz) almond macaroon biscuits,
    finely crushed*
parmesan cheese, finely grated

Originally built as a sixteenth century residence, the Gritti Palace Hotel in Venice is situated on the Grand Canal and faces the baroque church of Santa Maria della Salute. For sheer loveliness there are very few hotels in the world that can compete with this setting. Each year during the summer the Gritti holds cooking classes with guest demonstrators as well as recipes from its own kitchens. This was one of the unusual vegetables that was presented one year. It has a very slightly sweet flavour. It should really be served as a dish complete in itself, but if you wish to put it with meat, lamb or chicken are the best choice.

It is most important that when you buy the almond biscuits they are the bitter macaroons. These are the little, very hard and crisp biscuits much loved by Italians. I find these come in cellophane packets in most supermarkets.

Cut the ends from the zucchini. Cook zucchini in a large pot of salted water for a few minutes until they have just started to soften slightly. Remove and drain. Run cold water over them to stop them cooking any further. Cut into halves lengthwise and using a teaspoon remove the seeds. Turn the zucchini upside down to drain. Roughly chop the seeds and pulp taken from the centre.

Melt the butter in a frying pan and add the onion. Sauté, stirring occasionally until the onions are softened. Add the chopped seeds and pulp and cook until most of the moisture has evaporated. Place the onions and zucchini in a bowl.

Béchamel Sauce
Melt the butter and add the flour. Cook gently, stirring until the flour has cooked and is slightly granulated. Add the milk, stir until it comes to the boil. Cook gently for a couple of minutes and season with salt, pepper and a pinch of mustard.

This is only a small amount of sauce. It is used as a binding for the filling.

Mix the béchamel sauce with the onion and zucchini pulp in the bowl. Add the crushed almond biscuit crumbs. Using a spoon, fill the zucchini shells. Sprinkle a thin coating of the grated parmesan cheese over the top.

Place in one layer in a shallow ovenproof dish and bake in a moderate oven 180-190° C (350-375° F) for about 15 minutes or until the dish is piping hot and the cheese has melted.

Notes: It takes about 16 of the tiny almond macaroons to make sufficient crumbs for ½ cup.

Use parmesan and not some other cheese as the slight sharpness of this is a good contrast to the almond sweetness. For general notes on zucchinis see page 111.

Gritti' Stuffed Zucchini

ZUCCHINI COURGETTES

This is a vegetable which has gained a tremendous popularity over the last few years and is available for most of the year, varying in price according to the season. Zucchini should always be firm and glossy-skinned. The only disadvantage with this lovely and delicate vegetable is its high water content. Salting will draw out the water and then the zucchini can be patted dry. In recipes where it is grated, the zucchini is actually squeezed to remove the water and then left to dry on kitchen paper.

TOMATOES STUFFED WITH SPINACH

This dish looks very pretty and can be prepared well beforehand then cooked at dinner time. It is the type of vegetable dish which could be served as a course on its own. Fresh spinach is nicer than frozen, although I know it's tempting to use frozen because it's faster to prepare. However, it does not have enough texture for this dish.

Cut the tomatoes into halves, and using a teaspoon, scoop out the seeds. Season the inside with salt, pepper and a pinch of sugar and turn them upside down. They will drain this way.

Spinach Filling

Usually there is sufficient water on the leaves of the spinach for cooking. Remove any large stalks. Place the leaves in a large saucepan and add a little salt. Cook, stirring once or twice until it is just softened. This only takes a few minutes. Remove, drain well and then squeeze to remove all the moisture. Place the spinach down flat and cut or chop it a bit. It's easier to do this when it has cooled down a little.

Melt the butter in a frying pan. Add the onion and sauté, stirring occasionally until softened. Add the pine kernels to the pan and cook until they are coated with butter and very pale golden. Add the garlic, mix the spinach into this and stir to mix everything together well and then remove from the heat. Check the seasoning, you can add a little salt and pepper as needed. Fill the spinach into the tomatoes. Sprinkle the top of the spinach with the cheese.

Bake about 10 to 12 minutes in a moderate oven 180-190° C (350-375° F). The timing really depes on the season as tomatoes are much firmer in the winter.

Notes: The tomatoes can be prepared beforehand and the spinach filling cooked. They can be assembled an hour before baking but not much earlier or the filling will become wet as tomatoes give out juice.

INGREDIENTS
6 medium-sized ripe tomatoes
salt and pepper
a little sugar

SPINACH FILLING
1 bunch spinach, well washed
salt
60 g (2 oz) butter
1 white onion, finely diced
3 tablespoons pine kernels
1 clove garlic, crushed

TOPPING
3 tablespoons tasty cheese, grated

Rum and Almond Dessert Tart with Prunes (page 130)

GRATIN OF FENNEL

INGREDIENTS
3 whole fennel
water
salt
30 g (1 oz) butter
a little salt and pepper
2 tablespoons parmesan cheese, grated
1 tablespoon chicken stock

This lovely vegetable which has a very slight aniseed flavour is not used very much in cooking. I suspect this is because most people are not quite certain how to prepare it. You can see the white bulbs with the green feathery tips at various times in greengrocers, particularly those that have an Italian clientele.

Cut the feathery ends from the fennel and remove any very coarse outside sections. Cut it across into two or three slices, depending on the size.

Half fill a large frying pan with water and salt it. Bring to the boil. Place the fennel slices in one layer in the water and cook, turning once, until tender. You need to use an egg slice to turn them as they tend to come apart. Remove them and place on paper towelling to drain.

Butter a shallow ovenproof dish, large enough to hold them in one layer. Place them in the dish. Put a little piece of butter on top of each slice. Season. Sprinkle some parmesan cheese over this. Add the stock. Bake in a moderate oven 180-190° C (350-375° F) for about 20 minutes or until the top of the fennel is golden brown and glazed.

Notes: This is a vegetable which can be successfully reheated. To reheat, cook the fennel in the pan and place in the ovenproof dish with the butter and cheese and leave aside. Reheat later.

SAUTÉED GREEN VEGETABLES

INGREDIENTS
500 g (1 lb) zucchini
1 teaspoon salt
half a head of lettuce
1 bunch spinach, well washed
90 g (3 oz) butter
1 white onion, finely diced
¼ cup (2 fl oz) cream
extra salt and pepper as needed

A most interesting dish of sautéed greens, good with meats, particularly chicken or poultry, and reheats most successfully.

Discard the ends from the zucchini and grate the vegetable. Spread either in layers in a bowl, salting as you go or place it in the bowl, then salt and stir well. Leave to stand for 1 hour. Squeeze between your hands to extract most of the liquid and place on kitchen paper to dry.

Remove the white stalk from the lettuce, cut the leaves into thin strips. Remove the coarse stalks from the spinach and if the centre is coarse cut away. Cut large leaves in half.

In a large frying pan, melt a third of the butter and add the zucchini. Sauté until just softened. Remove to a bowl. Melt another third of the butter and add the onion and lettuce. Cook, giving it an occasional stir until tender and season with a little salt and pepper. Remove to the same bowl with the zucchini.

Melt the remaining third of butter and add the spinach. Cook quickly until just wilted and tender, seasoning with a little salt and pepper. Return the zucchini and lettuce to the pan, stir to mix and add the cream. Check the seasoning.

Notes: Keep refrigerated until you want to reheat this dish. It can either be reheated in a pan, or in a casserole in the oven, just be sure to give it an occasional stir.

TOMATOES

A smooth skinned, ripe, freshly picked tomato has to be one of the loveliest vegetables of all, but unfortunately, in the shops so often they seem to be little, hard, round, quite tasteless balls.

The ripeness and flavour of the tomatoes makes quite a difference to the recipe. They can often be improved by being stored at room temperature for a short time until they are red.

To Peel Tomatoes

For some of the dishes given it is necessary to peel the tomatoes. The easiest way is to cut a cross on the top, then drop them into boiling water. Put only two at a time in the water. Leave for about ten seconds and remove. The skin will have lifted slightly where you cut them and can easily be peeled back. Just watch that you don't leave them too long in the boiling water as the tomato starts to cook and becomes mushy.

TOMATOES WITH PINE KERNELS

This is a bright dish which looks good as an accompaniment to plain meats but is also flavoursome enough to be served as a small dish on its own, for example as a first course.

Cut the tomatoes into halves. Season the tops with salt, pepper and sugar.

Heat the butter in a frying pan. Add the tomatoes and cook for a minute on both sides. They should be still very firm but will be lightly coated with butter. Remove from the pan. Add the pine kernels to the same pan and cook, stirring until they are pale golden in colour.

Remove. Add the parsley and garlic and toss for a few seconds. Keep aside separately. Wipe out pan.

Melt the additional 45 g (1½ oz) butter and add the onion. Cook, stirring occasionally until it is softened. Mix this onion with the pine kernels.

To Assemble

Top the tomatoes first with a layer of the parsley and garlic mixture. Then press some of the onion and pine kernels on top of this. Place them in a shallow ovenproof dish and bake in a moderate oven 180-190° C (350-375° F) for 10 to 12 minutes or until just slightly softened.

There is no need to grease the baking dish beforehand as there will be sufficient butter on the tomatoes.

Notes: Although this may seem a fiddly dish it isn't really. The preparation is such that you can just keep using the same frying pan when you cook the different things. If however it starts to go a bit brown at any stage, you may need to rinse the pan and add a little extra piece of butter.

INGREDIENTS
6 medium-sized ripe tomatoes
salt and pepper
a little sugar
45 g (1½ oz) butter
3 tablespoons pine kernels
½ cup (¾ oz) parsley, finely chopped
2 cloves garlic, crushed
an additional 45 g (1½ oz) butter
1 white onion, finely diced

GRATED POTATO CASSEROLE

This dish is rich and buttery and can either be spooned from the casserole or cut into squares. It goes well with plain meats, but not meats which have a high fat content, such as pork or duck.

Peel the potatoes and grate them into a large bowl using a medium to coarse grater.

Add the milk, cheese, egg, onion, salt and pepper. Grease a baking or ovenproof dish which is shallow rather than deep and one which will hold about 6 cups (2½ pints). Place the potatoes in the dish. Dot the top with the little pieces of butter.

Cover the dish with some foil and bake in a moderate oven 180-190° C (350-375° F) for about 45 minutes or until the potato is softened. Then remove the foil and leave another 15 minutes until the top is a light golden colour.

Notes: This is the type of dish that, once cooked, can be kept warm for some time without spoiling. The preparation however is last minute, as grated potato browns easily. If you have a food processor, preparation is a lot faster. Although this dish can be made with new potatoes I find it becomes a bit starchy.

NEW POTATOES AND CAVIAR

INGREDIENTS
about 18 new baby potatoes
⅓ cup (2½ fl oz) sour cream
1 medium-sized white onion, finely diced
30 g (1 oz) pink caviar
1 tablespoon parsley, finely chopped
a little black pepper

You must use the tiny new potatoes for this. The combination of the slight saltiness of caviar is very good and goes well as an accompaniment to fish dishes.

Place the potatoes in a saucepan and cover with cold water. Salt. Cook until tender. Remove and drain. Peel away the skin.

Place the sour cream in the saucepan and add the potatoes, shake gently to warm them through a little. They should be just coated with the cream. Remove to a heated bowl.

Sprinkle white onion over the top, then the pink caviar, scatter this with a fork. Add parsley and black pepper. Don't toss the mixture, it mixes up quite well as it is served.

Note: Don't use black caviar in this dish. The dye which is used in the caviar gives an unpleasant grey look to the potatoes.

RICE AND PASTA

I haven't made any attempt to give a complete section on rice and pasta. Here are just three dishes which have been extremely popular in the cooking school. They are ideas upon which you can build to make endless variations.

RICE CREOLE STYLE

Heat the oil in a saucepan. Add the onion and green pepper and stirring occasionally, sauté until just softened.

Remove the onion and pepper but leave a little of the oil in the pan. Add the rice and stir. Cook until about half the rice grains are opaque. Add the tomatoes and fry a moment with the rice. Return the onion and pepper to the pan, add the stock, cayenne pepper and bring to the boil. Turn down the heat and leave to cook very gently for about 10 minutes.

Then place the ham on top and push this under the rice, using a fork. Either place in the oven to continue cooking, or cook again over a low heat until the rice is fluffy and all the liquid has been absorbed. This usually takes another 10 minutes or so.

Remove from the heat, add butter, stir gently and mix in the finely chopped parsley.

Notes: This dish has endless variations. You can add 500 g (1 lb) prawns; use green ones if possible, shell them then cut each into about 3 pieces. Add the prawns at the same time as you add the ham. They will steam through underneath the top of the rice. A dozen oysters are also delicious when added with the ham.

The dish should be slightly spicy. The cayenne should be enough to give it a bite. Salt is not added but this really depends on the saltiness of the chicken stock used. If your stock is undersalted then add a little salt to the rice before you place the lid on the pan.

INGREDIENTS
3 tablespoons oil
1 white onion, thinly sliced
1 green pepper, seeds removed, cut into long strips
1½ cups (7½ oz) long grain rice
250 g (8 oz) ripe tomatoes, peeled and diced
3 cups (1¼ pints) chicken stock
good pinch cayenne pepper
125 g (4 oz) ham, cut into thin strips
30 g (1 oz) butter
2 tablespoons parsley, finely chopped

RICE PILAF

A pilaf is one of the most useful of all rice dishes and if you stick to a few important points, it is virtually foolproof. It gives firm rice grains, is never gluey and is always perfectly cooked.

Heat the oil in a saucepan. Add the onion and rice. Cook, stirring until all the rice is well coated with oil and at least half of the rice grains have become opaque. Add the stock all at once. Because of the heat in the pan it will come to the boil within a minute.

Place a lid on the pan and cook, tightly covered and simmering gently for 12 to 15 minutes or until the rice is cooked and there is no liquid left in the pan. Season.

Remove from the heat, add the butter and stir until melted. If you want to keep this warm, place on the side of the stove and wrap a small towel around the pot to keep the warmth in. You can leave it for as long as 15 to 20 minutes.

Notes: All sorts of things can be added to Rice Pilaf. You can cook diced carrot or peas in with the rice, add a clove of crushed garlic to the onion and scatter parsley over the top when you serve it. Just remember that you always have double the quantity of stock to rice.

INGREDIENTS

2 tablespoons oil

1 medium-sized white onion, finely diced

2 cups (10 oz) long grain rice

4 cups (1½ pints) chicken stock (or beef stock for beef dishes)

salt and pepper, depending on the seasonings in the stock

60 g (2 oz) butter, cut in small pieces

TAGLIATELLE WITH SAUTÉED VEGETABLES

This is a very light dish, but should only be made when the vegetables are full of flavour and tomatoes are in season.

Peel the eggplant. Cut into slices and then into thin strips. Salt them and leave to stand for at least 30 minutes. Wash the zucchini, remove the ends and then grate the zucchini coarsely. Sprinkle with some salt, stir and leave to stand for about 30 minutes. Cut the tomatoes into small dice and leave aside. Wash the eggplant and pat dry. Melt the butter and oil in a frying pan and fry the eggplant quickly until it has just softened. Remove and leave in a bowl. Squeeze the zucchini dry. Place on paper towelling to drain. Add the zucchini to the same pan and fry until just tender. Remove and place with the eggplant in the bowl. Place the diced tomato in the pan, toss for only a minute. Mix with the other vegetables.

Cook the tagliatelle in a large pot of salted water until just tender. Remove and drain.

In a large saucepan or frying pan melt the additional butter, add garlic and tagliatelle, season and toss. Then add the cream, cheese and vegetables and stir until everything is heated through and the sauce is creamy. Serve immediately.

Note: This doesn't need any additional cheese, otherwise the taste will overpower the delicate flavour of the vegetables.

INGREDIENTS

1 small egplant, about 250 g (8 oz) in size

375 g (12 oz) zucchini

375 g (12 oz) tomatoes, peeled

salt

30 g (1 oz) butter

1 tablespoon oil

500 g (1 lb) tagliatelle, either white or green

60 g (2 oz) additional butter

1 clove garlic, crushed

¼ cup (2 fl oz) cream

3 tablespoons parmesan cheese, finely grated

SALADS

Brillat-Savarin declared that the purpose of a salad in dining was to freshen the palate. He was mainly talking about the salad which is dressed with oil and vinegar and is the classic accompaniment to freshen the palate after a main dish. The kinds of salads here fall more into the category of separate little courses, dishes which can also be served at parties or on a buffet. The Spinach Salad is probably the only one which could be classified as a green salad. The others are a little different from the usual selection, and are meant to be more of a separate course.

COLD POTATO SALAD WITH PINK CAVIAR

Under the vegetable section I have listed a recipe for a hot potato dish with sour cream and caviar (see p. 114). This recipe naturally altered a little, is also colourful and flavoursome when the potato is eaten as a salad.

Place the potatoes in a pot of salted water and cook until tender. Drain, leave to cool a little and remove the skins. Place potatoes in a bowl.

Mix the oil, vinegar, mayonnaise, salt and pepper with the onion. Shake or stir well. Pour over the potatoes while they are still warm. Leave aside to cool.

Before serving, scatter the caviar over the top and sprinkle with the parsley. This should be served at room temperature, never cold, and the salad is best served on the day it is made.

Note: Never use black caviar because the dye in it will turn the potatoes an unpleasant grey.

INGREDIENTS
18 small new potatoes

DRESSING
3 tablespoons oil
1 tablespoon white vinegar
2 tablespoons mayonnaise
salt and pepper
1 medium-sized white onion, finely diced

TO FINISH
1 x 30 g (1 oz) jar pink caviar
2 tablespoons parsley, finely chopped

SPINACH SALAD

This salad must be made with spinach, the tougher leaves and heavy stalks of silverbeet are unsuitable. When prepared carefully, spinach makes a really lovely salad.

Wash the spinach really well several times and leave to drain. Take hold of the end stalk with your hand and hold the leaf firmly with the other. Pull the stalk away so the entire length of it is removed. The smaller leaves can just have the main stalk cut. Then pat the spinach as dry as you can. Place in a bowl. Large leaves can be broken in two but leave the smaller ones whole.

Cut the boiled eggs into halves. Remove the yolks. Chop the whites into small strips. Sieve the yolks and leave on a plate.

INGREDIENTS
1 bunch spinach
2 hard boiled eggs

DRESSING
6 tablespoons oil
2 tablespoons white vinegar
or lemon juice
¼ teaspoon sugar
salt and pepper
pinch dry, English-style mustard

Dressing
Mix the dressing ingredients together and shake in a jar or stir well. Pour over the spinach and toss. Sprinkle the egg white around the edge of the bowl. Scatter the sieved yolk in centre.

Note: As size of bunches can vary, half a large bunch may suffice.

CUCUMBER AND LYCHEE SALAD

Tinned lychees are usually easily obtained or you may prefer to use grapes, when they are in season. The small white grapes are the best. If you use the larger ones you must remove all seeds.

Peel the cucumber. Cut in halves lengthwise. Using a teaspoon remove the seeds. Cut the cucumber into very thin slices.

Place in a bowl and sprinkle with salt, sugar and vinegar. Leave to stand for 1 hour. Remove from the bowl and drain well, pat the cucumber dry or squeeze a little. Place in a bowl and chill.

Just before serving, mix in the sour cream, mayonnaise, cayenne and stir. Add the lychees, cut in halves. Or add the grapes, whole if using sultana variety, cut if using larger grapes.

INGREDIENTS
1 large cucumber, or 2 small ones
½ teaspoon salt
1 teaspoon sugar
1 tablespoon white vinegar
1 tablespoon sour cream
1 tablespoon mayonnaise
pinch cayenne pepper
1 tin 450 g (1 lb) lychees
or 185 g (6 oz) white grapes

Note: Interesting with fish.

BEETROOT SALAD WITH ONIONS

Place the beetroot in a pan of salted water, cover and cook until quite tender. Drain and leave to cool slightly. Slip off the skins, roots and any stems. Cut the beetroot into even dice.

Mix together the sour cream, mayonnaise, salt, pepper, sugar and grated horseradish. Mix with the beetroot.

Heat the oil and add the onion. Sauté, stirring occasionally until the onion is softened. Before serving, warm the onion again and sprinkle over the top of the beetroot.

Notes: If you wish to produce even more flavour in the beetroot you can leave it to marinate. Save about a cup of the liquid when it is drained. Mix this liquid with ½ cup vinegar, 1 tablespoon sugar, and a little salt. Add the diced beetroot to this and keep refrigerated. It can be kept for days in this. Drain well before using the beetroot.

INGREDIENTS
3 medium-sized beetroot
⅓ cup (2½ fl oz) sour cream
2 tablespoons mayonnaise
salt and pepper
½ teaspoon sugar
2 teaspoons horseradish, grated
2 tablespoons oil
2 medium-sized onions, thinly sliced

ORANGE SALAD WITH RADISH DRESSING

Cut the skin away from the orange, removing most of the white part. Cut out the segments. Chill. Place the radishes in ice water to crisp them.

Dressing
Mix the oil, vinegar, paprika, salt, pepper and sugar together and leave at room temperature.

To Assemble the Salad
Place the orange segments on some lettuce leaves. Grate the radishes and mix with the dressing. Pour the dressing over the oranges. If you wish, sprinkle with spring onion.

Note: You can grate the radish beforehand if you wish but don't mix with the dressing until ready to serve as it tends to become a little bitter.

INGREDIENTS
6 medium-sized oranges
6 medium-sized radishes

DRESSING
6 tablespoons vegetable oil
2 tablespoons white vinegar
1 teaspoon paprika
  (use a sweet paprika not
  a hot one)
salt
white pepper
1 teaspoon sugar

lettuce leaves for serving
spring onion, finely chopped (optional)

GREEK SALAD

3 whole peppers (capsicum)
approximately ¼ cup (2 fl oz) olive oil
2 large white onions, thinly sliced
3 tomatoes
salt and pepper
pinch sugar

DRESSING
¼ cup (2 fl oz) olive or vegetable oil
2 tablespoons white vinegar
1 teaspoon lemon juice
½ teaspoon sugar
1 teaspoon dry, English-style mustard
salt and pepper

some lettuce leaves

The ingredients for this salad are first cooked in oil. This brings out quite a different flavour.

Cut the ends from the peppers. Cut into halves and remove the seeds. Place on a scone tray and put under a pre-heated griller until the skin is dark brown and puffed. Remove and leave to cool. Peel the outside skin, or as much of it as you can. It will be like tissue paper. Cut the pepper into strips and leave aside.

Heat a little oil in a frying pan. Add the sliced onion and sauté, stirring occasionally until softened but not golden. Remove.

Peel the tomatoes by plunging them into boiling water for about 30 seconds and then removing the skins. Cut them into halves or thirds if large. Add a little more oil to the same pan and add the tomatoes. Season them with salt and pepper and the sugar. Turn once and season the other side. Remove and leave to cool. Don't overcook the tomatoes, they should be fried for only about a minute each side so they remain firm inside.

Dressing
Mix all the dressing ingredients together and shake well or stir with a fork until thickened.

To Assemble
Place the lettuce leaves on a platter and arrange the tomatoes on top. Scatter the onion and pepper over this and then pour the dressing over the top.

Note: This salad is good as an accompaniment to steaks or veal dishes such as schnitzel.

APPLE SALAD

You can peel the apples or leave the skin on for colour.

Core them and cut into neat dice. Cover with the lemon juice, sugar, salt and stir. This will prevent any discoloration. Add the onion, Tabasco and green pepper.

Place the coconut into a small saucepan and add the milk. Bring the milk to the boil. Remove from the heat and stand for about 10 minutes. Drain the coconut but don't press all the moisture out of it. Mix this moist coconut milk into the apple.

Notes: This apple salad will keep for 24 hours. If it tastes too acidic because of the lemon juice, add a little more sugar and salt to counteract this.

This salad is especially good after pork dishes.

INGREDIENTS
3 eating apples
2 tablespoons lemon juice
2 teaspoons sugar
pinch salt
1 medium-sized white onion, finely diced
few drops Tabasco
1 small green pepper, ends removed, seeds taken out and cut into small dice
3 tablespoons desiccated coconut
½ cup (4 fl oz) milk

PASTA SALAD

This may sound strange but it is a very tasty salad and good for a buffet or party. If you serve it to accompany a dish, it is best with steak or veal. The most successful pasta for this is either a macaroni, spaghetti or small shell pasta. If you use a variety which is large, the flavourings of the dressing won't soak in and it will be a little tasteless.

If you use spaghetti, break the strands up into short lengths.

Cook the pasta in a large pot of salted, boiling water until just tender. Drain well and let stand for a couple of minutes.

Dressing

Mix the oil, vinegar, garlic and mayonnaise with salt and pepper and mix this through the warm pasta. Let stand for about 30 minutes before serving.

To Assemble

Mix all ingredients into the pasta dish. Stand for about 1 hour.

Note: The most important thing is to mix the dressing into the warm spaghetti. It will look rather wet but it soaks up the dressing as it cools. The salad can be eaten within an hour of making it, but it keeps well for 12 hours.

INGREDIENTS
250 g (8 oz) pasta

DRESSING
6 tablespoons olive oil
2 tablespoons white vinegar
1 clove garlic, crushed
1 tablespoon mayonnaise
salt and pepper

TO ASSEMBLE
125 g (4 oz) ham, cut in thin strips
2 tomatoes, peeled and diced small
2 hard boiled eggs, cut into small pieces
3 tablespoons parsley, finely chopped

Beautifully prepared desserts give a very special finish to any dinner, even very simple desserts. Fresh fruits of the season are one of the nicest. Such fruits as perfumed raspberries or strawberries, ripe peaches or a bowl of chilled cherries are all excellent choices, especially if the meal has been rich. However for the times when you want to prepare a dessert I have included a variety; there are some dessert tarts; hot and cold desserts; and a section on home-made frozen desserts and ice creams.

The cakes in the section are dessert cakes meant to be served either as an alternative to a dessert or with coffee.

APPLE AND MINCE TART

Often a plain mince tart is a little rich at the end of a meal but this one has apple added which makes a much lighter mixture.

See general notes on handling pastry (p. 45).

Pastry Case
Sift the flour, salt and icing sugar together. Add the ground almonds and mix through. Add the butter and work into the mixture until it is crumbly. Then add the egg yolk and lemon juice and knead lightly until it is smooth.

Chill for about 1 hour, or you can roll it out and then chill. Fit into a flan tin with a removable base. Press on to the sides and prick the base with a fork. Butter a double thickness of greaseproof paper on one side. Set buttered side down in the pastry shell. Fill with dry beans, such as haricot or kidney beans and bake in a moderate oven 180-190° C (350-375° F) for about 20 minutes or until the shell is set. Remove the paper, leave case to dry for a few minutes in the oven. Don't let it brown too much as this case will be cooked again with a filling in it.

Filling
Peel and core the apples and cut into thin slices. Place the butter and sugar in a saucepan and cook until the butter has melted. Place the apples on top and stir to coat the slices with butter. Place a lid on the saucepan and cook, shaking or stirring occasionally until the apples are soft. Then remove the lid and if they are wet and there is a lot of liquid in the saucepan, cook over fairly high heat until it has nearly all evaporated. Watch that it doesn't catch on the base.

Remove the apples to a bowl and stir with a wooden spoon to break them up well. There isn't any need to purée or sieve these. Add the grated orange rind, cinnamon and fruit mince. Mix the cornflour with the brandy and add to apples and stir well.

Pour this mixture into the pre-baked pastry case. Place into a moderate oven 180-190° C (350-375° F) and cook until it is firm to touch on top. It usually takes about 25 minutes for the filling to set.

Remove and leave to cool.

INGREDIENTS

PASTRY

to make a tart case 25 cm (10 in)
1 cup (4 oz) flour
pinch salt
2 tablespoons icing sugar
¼ cup (2 oz) ground almonds
90 g (3 oz) butter, cut into small pieces
1 egg yolk
1 tablespoon lemon juice

FILLING

500 g (1 lb) green apples
60 g (2 oz) butter
⅓ cup (2½ oz) sugar
rind of 1 orange, grated
¼ teaspoon cinnamon
1 cup (10 oz) fruit mince
2 teaspoons cornflour
2 tablespoons brandy

PEAR GARNISH

2 large firm eating pears
¼ cup (2 fl oz) water
¼ cup (2 oz) sugaro
30 g (1 oz) butter

GLAZE

⅓ cup (3½ oz) apricot jam
1 tablespoon brandy

Notes: This tart can be reheated most successfully and keeps for several days. It can be served just as it is or decorated with pears. The pear garnish takes a little time but looks most attractive and can either be done as soon as you make the tart or placed on top shortly before serving.

Pear Garnish

Peel the pears, core them and slice thinly. Place the water, sugar and butter in a small saucepan and cook until the butter has melted. Add the sliced pears, stir to coat with the liquid so that they won't brown. Cook very gently without a lid until they are slightly glazed. If they aren't soft, place a lid on the pan for a few minutes and this will soften them. Remove from the saucepan, place on a plate and leave to cool.

To Decorate

Arrange the pears around the edge of the tart, slightly overlapping. Then arrange one or two slices inside this to make an even edge in the centre.

Glaze

Heat the jam and brandy in a small saucepan. Cook a couple of minutes. Push through a sieve and brush this over the top of the pears to glaze them. Leave to set.

There is no need to keep this tart refrigerated, just keep in a cool place. Don't place in a tin or container as it will become wet.

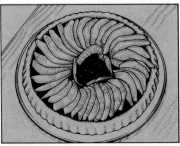

When the tart is cooked, arrange the sliced pears around the edge, slightly overlapping. To make the centre edge even, place some more slices of pear to form a circle.

INGREDIENTS

LEMON PASTRY

*Makes enough for a 25 cm (10 in) base,
    rolled thinly*

1 cup (4 oz) plus 2 tablespoons flour
90 g (3 oz) butter, cut into small pieces
2 tablespoons castor sugar
2 egg yolks
rind of 1 lemon, grated
1 or 2 teaspoons lemon juice as needed

LEMON SOUFFLÉ

4 egg yolks
½ cup (3½ oz) castor sugar
rind of 2 lemons, grated
½ cup (4 fl oz) lemon juice
2 egg whites
additional ¼ cup (2 oz) castor sugar

GLAZE

½ cup (5 oz) apricot jam
1 tablespoon brandy

LEMON SOUFFLÉ TART

This pastry has a lemon soufflé baked inside. It is very easy to do, and is equally delicious warm or cold. As the soufflé cools it makes a soft filling.

Sift the 1 cup (4 oz) and 2 tablespoons flour into a bowl. Add the butter pieces. Crumble the butter using your fingertips until all the mixture is crumbly and then add the castor sugar, mixing with a fork.

Place the egg yolks, lemon rind and 1 teaspoon of the lemon juice in the centre. Extra lemon can be added as needed. Gradually work the flour mixture in and then knead. If it looks dry, sprinkle the extra lemon juice over the top. Mix until it is smooth. You can chill this if it is a little sticky although usually it is easy to handle.

Roll this out between paper and make into a circle just slightly larger than the tin. Bake in a flan tin with a removable base. Pre-baking ensures a shell which has a crisp base, but as it is going to be cooked again with a filling, pre-bake it until only light golden in colour.

Form the pastry into the shell and press on the edges. Prick the base with a fork. If you didn't refrigerate the pastry before rolling you can now chill for about 20 minutes.

Butter a double thickness of greaseproof paper and place butter side down in the pastry shell. Fill with dried beans, such as haricot beans or kidney beans. Bake in a moderate oven 180-190° C (350-375° F) for about 20 to 25 minutes until the shell is set, then remove the paper and beans and return to the oven for a few minutes to dry the shell. Remove. Leave to cool.

When making this tart I found that if I put the soufflé in the tart base while it was hot it puffed too much and cracked all over the top. The tart base can be tepid when you use it, but not hot.

Lemon Soufflé

Place the egg yolks, castor sugar, lemon rind and lemon juice in a small saucepan and mix well. Then place over the heat and using a small whisk, stir constantly until it has thickened. This mustn't boil. Watch, as it only takes a few minutes to cook. Remove from the heat and place in a bowl. Cool, stirring a couple of times.

While the lemon base is cooling, beat the egg whites until stiff. Add the additional castor sugar and beat again until very stiff. Add the lemon base to the egg whites, a spoonful at a time very gently folding it through. Then pour this into the pre-baked tart case.

Place back in the moderate oven and cook until the top is puffed and firm to touch. It usually takes about 18 to 20 minutes. The top will be quite a deep golden brown but the soufflé must be well cooked otherwise it collapses very quickly and shrinks away from the sides of the pastry.

Remove from oven. It will now look puffed and high. Place aside. This tart can be eaten hot if you wish although it is just as good cold, or even reheated for 5 minutes and served warm. It won't puff again though, even if you reheat it. Naturally as it stands, the soufflé deflates and will end up level with the top of the pastry crust.

This can be glazed, if you wish, with some apricot jam for a shiny surface.

Glaze

Place the jam and brandy in a small saucepan and heat. Cook for about 5 minutes until it is slightly thickened. Push through a sieve so it is completely smooth. Using a pastry brush, cover the surface of the tart.

Notes: This tart is nicest eaten within 24 hours of being made.

LEMON TART

Lemon is probably one of the most popular of all flavours. This tart has a creamy filling, and is nicest served with slightly sweetened cream and with berry fruits.

Sift the flour and salt into a basin, add the castor sugar and stir in. Add the butter pieces and mix with your fingertips until the mixture is crumbly and the butter is reduced to tiny bits.

Place the egg yolk and lemon juice in the centre and work the flour into this. Then turn out and knead lightly until it forms a soft ball. If too firm you can sprinkle a few drops more lemon juice over the top. You can chill or roll it out first and then chill in the case.

Roll out between paper and make into a circle slightly larger than the tin. Mould and press the pastry into the tin. Prick the pastry lightly but not right through. Bake blind in a flan tin with a removable base with paper and beans in a moderate oven 180-190° C (350-375° F) for about 20 to 25 minutes or until golden. Remove paper and beans, leave case to dry for a few minutes in the oven. Remove and cool slightly.

Lemon Filling

Place the eggs and castor sugar in a small bowl and beat until light in colour. Add the lemon rind, lemon juice, orange juice and mix. Melt the butter in a small saucepan and mix through. Pour this mixture into the case and return to the oven to cook. It should be just set when cooked and be a golden colour on top. This usually takes about 15 to 20 minutes.

Notes: This tart keeps for about 3 days and can be reheated when you wish. When it is cooked a certain amount of butter will sometimes form underneath the flan tin. It doesn't detract from the taste but it tends to form a sticky mixture which caramelises with the lemon. This makes the tart stick once it goes cold, so just loosen slightly from the flan tin whilst still warm and then it will be easier to cut.

INGREDIENTS
PASTRY
Makes enough for a 25 cm (10 in) base

1½ cups (6 oz) flour
pinch salt
2 tablespoons castor sugar
125 g (4 oz) butter, cut into small pieces
1 egg yolk
1 tablespoon lemon juice

LEMON FILLING
3 eggs
¾ cup (5 oz) castor sugar
grated rind of 2 lemons
4 tablespoons lemon juice
⅓ cup (2½ fl oz) orange juice
60 g (2 oz) butter

PEAR TART

INGREDIENTS

FILLING

1 kg (2 lbs) rather firm eating pears
3 cups (1¼ pints) light red wine
½ cup (3½ oz) sugar
rind of 1 orange, grated

TO FINISH

3 teaspoons gelatine
¼ cup (2 fl oz) water
a little lemon juice (optional)

TO ASSEMBLE

½ cup (5 oz) apricot jam
pears
syrup

SOUR CREAM SAUCE TO SERVE WITH PEAR TART

½ cup (4 fl oz) thick or pure cream
¼ cup (2 fl oz) sour cream
¼ cup icing sugar
rind of 1 lemon, grated
good pinch nutmeg
¼ teaspoon cinnamon

Make up one pastry case, using the Lemon Pastry from the Lemon Soufflé Tart (p.124).

Pre-bake and allow to become quite golden as this tart will not be cooked again.

Peel the pears and cut them into quarters. Remove the core.

Heat the red wine, sugar and grated rind of orange and add the pears. Cover the saucepan, cook, stirring them gently in the beginning so they are well coated with wine. The longer they take to cook, the better the flavour will be, so leave them to cook very slowly. They take about 45 minutes to 1 hour, depending on their ripeness. When cooked, leave to cool in the syrup.

Drain, placing the pear sections on some paper towelling so that they are as dry as possible.

Return the syrup to a saucepan and boil rapidly without a lid until it has been reduced to one cup.

Mix the gelatine and water, add to the hot syrup and stir to dissolve. Leave the syrup aside until it begins to thicken. If you find it too sweet you can add some lemon juice. You can refrigerate if it takes too long to thicken and you are ready to assemble.

To Assemble

Heat the apricot jam in a small saucepan and then cook until slightly thickened. Watch that it doesn't burn. Remove and push through a sieve over the base of the pre-baked pastry case and spread with a pastry brush to coat the base and sides. Leave to set for a few minutes.

Place the pears in the pastry case, overlapping them slightly. Have the top towards the centre. There will be a gap in the centre. Keep aside one or two and place them neatly to fill the gap. Spoon the syrup over the top of the pears. It will be dark burgundy in colour by now. The top of the tart must be completely coated with this glaze. Refrigerate until set.

Serve with Sour Cream Sauce.

Notes: While the pears are cooking in the red wine there will be quite a bit of scum around the edges of the pan. Disregard this as it cooks away. The most important thing is to be careful that the glaze is thick enough when you pour it over the top of the pears, otherwise it soaks into the pastry and makes it really soggy.

This type of fruit tart is nicest eaten the day it is made, however you can make it about lunchtime for a dinner in the evening. The pastry case can be made the day before and the pears keep successfully for several days in the syrup, so you can assemble it the day it is to be eaten.

Sour Cream Sauce

Stir all the ingredients together. Chill for at least 4 hours.

This cream is served from a jug. If you wish to serve it a little firmer, whisk lightly for just a minute so that it holds a shape.

It keeps well for days in the refrigerator, covered.

Notes: This cream can be served with any fruit tarts and is excellent with plain cooked fruits.

Orange Meringue Crown with Strawberries (page 134)

APPLE TART WITH ORANGE GLAZE

This is an interesting apple tart. The orange glaze is really like an orange-flavoured royal icing which is baked on top and forms a crust.

Sift the flour and salt into a basin. Add the castor sugar and mix with the lemon and orange rinds and cinnamon. Cut the butter into small dice and add. Work with your fingers until the mixture is crumbly. Then add egg yolks and work into a soft dough. If too dry, add a little lemon juice as you go. You can either chill this base or roll out immediately and then chill.

Divide the pastry, keep one-third for the top and use the remaining two-thirds for the base. Roll out and place into a flan tin 25 cm (10 in) in size. Use one with a removable base. Chill for 20 minutes if you didn't chill the pastry before rolling.

Filling and Glaze for Base
Place the breadcrumbs either in a dry frying pan and heat until dry and pale golden or place them on a tray in the oven. Do not let them go brown.

Heat the apricot jam until bubbling, cook one minute and then spread this over the base of the pastry. Sprinkle the crumbs over the jam in the base.

Apple Filling
Place the butter and sugar in a saucepan and warm until the butter is melted. Add the apples, jam, lemon rind and spices and stir for a moment to coat the apples with the mixture. Cover and cook until the apples are soft. Turn up the heat, remove the lid and cook the apples until dry, stirring. Remove and leave to cool. Place the apples in the tart case.

Roll out the remaining pastry and fit over the top. Pinch the edges together to join the base.

Orange Glaze
Mix the egg white, unbeaten, with the orange rind and icing sugar. Stir for a moment until smooth. This will be fairly liquid. Then spread it over the pastry top. Scatter the almonds over this.

Place into a moderate oven 180-190° C (350-375° F) for about 35 minutes or until the pastry is cooked and the topping is golden. If the top appears to be going too dark, cover loosely with a piece of foil.

Remove and serve warm or leave to go cold and serve with some lightly whipped cream.

Notes: The tart can be reheated if you wish, but because apples have a certain amount of moisture, eventually the pastry will soften. The tart, however, will keep for 24 to 36 hours.

Although it may read as a lengthy recipe, the apple filling can be prepared well beforehand and kept refrigerated for days. The pastry also can be chilled or frozen.

INGREDIENTS

PASTRY
1¾ cups (7 oz) flour
pinch salt
⅓ cup (2½ oz) castor sugar
rind of 1 lemon, grated
rind of 1 orange, grated
¼ teaspoon cinnamon
125 g (4 oz) butter
2 egg yolks
lemon juice if needed

FILLING AND GLAZE FOR BASE
2 tablespoons breadcrumbs made from stale bread
⅓ cup (3½ oz) apricot jam

APPLE FILLING
30 g (1 oz) butter
½ cup (3½ oz) sugar
1 kg (2 lbs) green apples, peeled, cored and thinly sliced
2 tablespoons apricot jam
rind of 1 lemon, grated
good pinch cinnamon
good pinch nutmeg

ORANGE GLAZE
1 egg white
rind of 1 orange, grated
1 cup (5 oz) icing sugar
2 tablespoons flaked almonds

Chocolate Fondant (page 132)

RUM AND ALMOND DESSERT TART WITH PRUNES

INGREDIENTS

PASTRY

to make a tart case 25 cm (10 in)

1 cup (4 oz) plain flour
pinch salt
2 tablespoons castor sugar
60 g (2 oz) butter, cut into small pieces
1 egg yolk
2 tablespoons lemon juice

PRUNE MIXTURE

250 g (8 oz) prunes
30 g (1 oz) butter
2 tablespoons castor sugar
¼ cup (2 fl oz) brown rum

REMAINING MIXTURE

125 g (4 oz) butter
⅓ cup (2½) oz castor sugar
1 tablespoon cornflour
3 eggs
¼ cup (2 fl oz) cream
rind of 1 lemon, grated
1 tablespoon lemon juice
½ cup (1¾ oz) ground almonds
¼ teaspoon almond essence

TO FINISH

icing sugar

Of all the tarts that I have ever demonstrated this has been one of the most popular. It is one of Julia Child's recipes and I came across this in San Francisco where it was published for the San Francisco Museum of Art. Famous for her television programme and cookery books, Julia Child is a much-loved and very important part of the cooking scene in America.

Sift the flour and salt into a large bowl. Add the castor sugar and mix. Add the butter and work it into the flour until the mixture is crumbly. Then add the egg yolk and lemon juice and knead lightly until smooth. You can chill for about 20 minutes if the mixture is sticky.

Roll out into the tart base. Press on to the sides and prick the base with a fork. If you didn't refrigerate the pastry before rolling you can now chill the tart base for about 20 minutes.

Butter a double thickness of greaseproof paper, or you can use foil. Set buttered side down in the pastry shell. Fill with dried beans, such as haricot beans or kidney beans. Bake in a moderate oven 180-190° C (350-375° F) for about 20 to 25 minutes or until the shell is set. Remove paper and beans and leave case to dry for a few minutes in the oven. Do not let it go brown as it will be cooked again for some time with the filling.

Prune Mixture

Place the prunes in a small basin and pour boiling water over the top to cover them. Stand for 1 minute. Drain. Remove the stones, chop each prune into halves or thirds. Heat the butter and castor sugar in a frying pan. Cook gently for a couple of minutes until the sugar has melted. Add the prunes and cook until slightly golden and well coated with glaze. Add the rum, turn the heat low and leave to cook for a couple of minutes.

Remove to a bowl and let cool.

Remaining Mixture

Cream the butter and sugar until quite fluffy. Add the cornflour and then the eggs, one at a time. Add cream, lemon rind, lemon juice, ground almonds and almond essence. If the mixture curdles, stand the bowl in warm water for a moment and beat well with a wooden spoon. It should be smooth and creamy. Then add the prunes last and mix through.

Place the mixture into the pastry case and put onto a scone tray. Then sift a generous layer of icing sugar over the top, through a fine sieve. Place in moderate oven 180-190° C (350-375° F) for about 25 to 30 minutes or until the tart is puffed and set on top.

Remove and leave to cool.

Notes: This tart keeps particularly well for 3 or 4 days. You can sift a little more icing sugar over the top before serving and it can be warmed again for about 8 minutes if you wish. It is good with a bowl of lightly whipped, very slightly sweetened cream.

GRAND MARNIER MOULD WITH HOT STRAWBERRY SAUCE

This is a rich custard flavoured with liqueur and lightened with cream. It can be set in a bowl but looks attractive in a soufflé dish. However, so that it will come above the edge of the dish you must use a very small one. Set in something like a savarin tin or jelly mould it looks nice. It is firm enough to unmould yet very light to eat.

Place the milk in a saucepan and heat until it is almost boiling. Place the egg yolks in a basin, add the sugar and beat until light. Tip the hot milk into the egg mixture and mix well. Return the entire mixture to the saucepan and cook, stirring with a whisk rather than a wooden spoon to keep the mixture moving. (You could use a double boiler for this custard — it is safer, but is also tedious and slow.) Be careful not to let it come to the boil. This can be prevented by lifting the saucepan and whisking if it looks like becoming too hot.

When the custard has thickened (it will only be a very light custard) remove from the heat. This takes only a few minutes to thicken as the milk was already hot.

Mix the gelatine with water and stir. Place this over hot water in a small bowl or stand the gelatine in a cup in a saucepan of water and heat until dissolved.

Mix the gelatine into the custard, stir. Add the vanilla and liqueur and pour into a basin to cool. Leave, stirring occasionally, until quite cold.

Have the cream lightly whipped so it holds only soft peaks; stiffly whipped cream doesn't fold in so evenly. Fold through the custard. Pour this into a mould which will hold about 4 cups (1½ pints), or make a soufflé type of dessert but the soufflé dish should be a 3 cup (1¼ pints) size. If you use a mould, don't oil it. Just rinse out with cold water before adding the custard. Chill for several hours.

Dip the mould into warm water and turn out on a plate. If you are keeping it for any length of time, cover the top with plastic wrap.

Note: If this is well covered it will keep for 36 hours.

Strawberry Sauce

Melt the butter and add the sugar. Cook a couple of minutes. The sugar may look granulated as it cooks, but don't let it go brown. Add the red currant jelly and liqueur and stir to dissolve the sugar and the red currant jelly.

Cut the strawberries into slices. Add and simmer for about 1 minute or until they are heated through.

Note: Strawberries become very acid when they are cooked for too long, so never overheat them. If you wish, the sauce can be made beforehand and reheated, but only add the strawberries when you reheat it.

INGREDIENTS
3 cups (1¼ pints) milk
5 egg yolks
5 tablespoons sugar
1 tablespoon and 2 teaspoons gelatine
¼ cup (2 fl oz) water
1 teaspoon vanilla
4 tablespoons Grand Marnier
½ cup (4 fl oz) cream, lightly whipped

STRAWBERRY SAUCE
This sauce can also be served with any vanilla flavoured dessert or a plain vanilla soufflé.

60 g (2 oz) butter
3 tablespoons sugar
⅓ cup (3½ oz) red currant jelly
⅓ cup (2½ fl oz) orange-flavoured liqueur
1 punnet strawberries, hulled

CHOCOLATE FONDANT

INGREDIENTS
¼ cup (2 fl oz) milk
125 g (4 oz) dark chocolate
60 g (2 oz) unsalted butter
1 teaspoon instant coffee
4 egg yolks
4 egg whites
¾ cup (4 oz) icing sugar
1 tablespoon brandy

DECORATION
1 cup (8 fl oz) cream
1 tablespoon icing sugar
1 teaspoon vanilla
60 g (2 oz) dark chocolate

This dessert is made rather like a chocolate soufflé but is then left to go cold. It is very moist and light. You make it in a soufflé dish, so it rises up and forms a round cake shape. Use a soufflé dish which holds about 5 cups (2 pints) and brush with butter inside. Use a sheet of foil which will encircle the dish by 1½ times and fold it over lengthwise. Brush one side of the foil with butter. Place around dish, buttered side in, so the collar is well above the dish. Tie with string. Make sure the string is close to the top of the dish to support the soufflé.

Place the milk in a small saucepan and warm. Break the chocolate into squares and add to the milk. Cook over low heat, stirring occasionally until the chocolate is melted and smooth. Remove from the heat.

Cut the butter into about 8 pieces and add these, a couple at a time, stirring until melted and smooth. Add the instant coffee and then egg yolks, one at a time.

Beat the egg whites in a bowl until they hold stiff peaks. Add the icing sugar and beat again until very stiff. Transfer the chocolate mixture to a bowl. Add the egg whites, one-third at a time, folding them in.

Add brandy with the last portion of egg white.

Pour the chocolate mixture into the dish. Stand in a baking dish about half filled with water, and bake in a moderate oven 180-190° C (350-375° F) for about 45 minutes or until firm to touch. After about 25 to 30 minutes have a look at the soufflé; if the top is becoming too brown, cover lightly with some foil. This chocolate dish tends to become too hard on top. It is a little difficult to really tell when it is cooked but it doesn't matter so long as it is lightly set.

Remove from the oven and leave to cool in the dish. It will deflate as it cools. When cold, run a knife around the edge and turn out gently onto a plate. Cover and refrigerate.

Notes: When making this dish sometimes the soufflé cracks on top. This doesn't matter at all as this top will eventually be the base when it is turned out. For easier turning out, line the inside base of the soufflé dish with a circle of buttered foil.

Decoration

Whip the cream until it is stiff, mix in the icing sugar and vanilla and beat again. Keep cold.

Place the chocolate in a basin and stand this in a pan of water. Heat the pan until the chocolate is softened, stir and then mix well until smooth and shiny and quite warm.

Place a sheet of greaseproof or wax paper on a board. Place the base of the soufflé dish on top of this and draw around to make the same sized circle. Then place the warm chocolate in a cone made from paper or use a piping bag with a plain tube. Cut the end of the paper. Pipe around the circle first, then lattice across the centre of the circle.

Refrigerate to set.

Very carefully peel the paper from the lattice. Cover the top of the cake with about half of the cream. Place the remainder of the cream in a piping bag with a star tube. Pipe a layer of rosettes around the edge of the dessert. Place the chocolate lattice so it rests on the cream. Then pipe another layer of rosettes around the edge. The lattice will appear slightly suspended in the centre. If this sounds difficult I can assure you it isn't really. The whole thing takes only a couple of minutes to do and it looks quite spectacular. You can use the lattice method to decorate cakes or desserts of any description.

Notes: The chocolate dessert can be made and kept well covered for 24 hours before decorating. Once decorated, serve within about 6 to 8 hours.

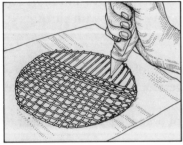

1. Place a sheet of waxed greaseproof paper on a board and mark a circle.

2. Melted chocolate is piped around the edge of the circle and then latticed.

ORANGE CREAM

Orange Cream can be served plain or with fruits in season. It is particularly good with sliced oranges or berry fruits.

Mix the egg yolks with the castor sugar in a basin and beat until slightly pale in colour. Add the lemon juice, white wine and orange juice and mix. Place this in a saucepan and cook, stirring all the time until it has lightly thickened. Cooking directly over the heat is much quicker than using a double boiler, although a double boiler is safer. However as long as you constantly stir and don't let the mixture boil, it will be fine. Often a small whisk is even better than a spoon.

When lightly thickened, remove from the heat and leave to cool, stirring occasionally. Add vanilla, then orange-flavoured liqueur and cream. Chill well.

Notes: This is a light mixture in texture and improves by being made 24 hours before you eat it. It keeps well for about 5 days, however it may be best to keep it covered in the refrigerator.

INGREDIENTS
5 egg yolks
6 tablespoons castor sugar
2 tablespoons lemon juice
4 tablespoons dry white wine
1 cup (4 fl oz) orange juice, strained
½ teaspoon vanilla
2 tablespoons orange-flavoured liqueur
½ cup (4 fl oz) thick or pure cream

FRUIT SALAD

INGREDIENTS

1 punnet strawberries

3 oranges

2 fresh mangoes sliced, or 1 tin mangoes,
(about 450 g drained

SYRUP

1 orange

1 lemon

¾ cup (5 oz) sugar

1½ cups (12 fl oz) water

The fruits in this can be varied, however usually 3 are sufficient. The syrup can be made and kept refrigerated for about 5 days and then used as you wish.

Hull the strawberries. Place in a bowl. Cut the rind and the white part from the orange. Remove the segments using a small sharp knife. Add the mango. Stir gently.

Syrup

Using a vegetable peeler, peel the orange thinly. Peel the lemon. Place the strips down on a board on top of each other and cut into very thin strips.

Place the sugar and water in a saucepan and heat until the sugar is dissolved. Add the strips of rind. Cook gently until the rind is quite tender. If the syrup starts to reduce too much, place a lid on the pan. When the rind is tender, remove and cool. The rind will have flavoured the syrup very lightly with citrus.

To Serve

An hour beforehand, add just a little of the syrup with a few strips of peel to the fruit. Refrigerate, stirring once or twice. Serve really cold.

You can also add a tablespoon of orange-flavoured liqueur to the fruit if you wish.

ORANGE MERINGUE CROWN WITH STRAWBERRIES

INGREDIENTS

MERINGUE

4 egg whites

pinch salt

8 tablespoons (absolutely flat) of castor
sugar

ORANGE CREAM

2 cups (16 fl oz) pure cream (it is essential
to use pure cream for this as other
creams won't remain stiff when you add
the liquid)

rind of 1 large orange, grated

2 tablespoons castor sugar

⅓ cup (2½ fl oz) orange juice

3 tablespoons orange-flavoured liqueur

STRAWBERRY MIXTURE

1 punnet strawberries, hulled

2 tablespoons Orange Cream

This dish is a matter of assembling together different things which taste good and the way it is presented makes a beautiful dessert. The various stages: meringues, strawberries, an orange-flavoured cream can easily be prepared beforehand. The dish can be prepared a couple of hours before serving.

Beat the egg whites with a pinch of salt until they are stiff. Gradually add the castor sugar and beat until the mixture is glossy and holds very stiff peaks. Using a spoon about the size of a dessert spoon, make small mounds on a well-buttered tray. You can pipe little mounds out if you find this quicker but don't make them any more than 2.5 cm (1 in) in size.

Place them in a slow oven 140° C (275° F) until they are firm and dry. Try not to make them golden, keep them as white as possible and if they start to colour turn the oven off. They will take several hours to dry out. When cooked, remove and loosen from the tray. Leave to cool and store in an air-tight tin.

Makes about 36 meringues.

Orange Cream

Beat the cream until it holds stiff peaks. Make sure it is very cold when you beat so it won't go buttery. Add the rind of orange and the castor sugar and stir. Then gradually add the orange juice, whisking as you go so the cream doesn't become watery. Finally add the liqueur. Keep chilled until ready to use.

Strawberry Mixture

Mix the strawberries with 2 tablespoons of Orange Cream and keep cold.

To Assemble

Select a large platter about 30 cm (12 in) in diameter. Spread a thin layer of the Orange Cream over the base.

Arrange a circle of the meringues around the edge of the platter. Fill the centre with the Strawberry Mixture.

Keep aside about 3 or 4 meringues which will be used for the top. Pair the others together with a generous spoonful of the Orange Cream. Using more Cream to hold them, place these over the berries and around the edges so they rise like a little pyramid, completely covering the strawberries. Then place a little Orange Cream on the top and use the other 3 or 4 meringues to form a little peak.

Place this in the refrigerator while the chocolate is prepared.

Melt the butter in a small saucepan. Break the dark chocolate into pieces and add to the butter. Remove from the heat and stir until it is melted and smooth. The addition of butter makes the chocolate runnier and gives the right effect to finish this dessert.

Place the chocolate in a paper cone and cut away the end or place in a piping bag with a plain tube. Remove the meringue from the refrigerator. Hold the piping bag or cone above the meringue and moving your hands up and down quickly pipe all around so the chocolate forms little lines and little melted pieces all over the outside. Then chill this for the chocolate to set.

Note: Although I have mentioned that this should be made about 2 hours beforehand sometimes it isn't possible to do such a last minute job. The dessert still tastes delicious even as long as 12 hours after making it, but the taste is different. The meringue becomes softened and is flavoured more with orange.

TO ASSEMBLE
Meringue
Orange Cream
Strawberry Mixture
15 g (½ oz) butter, preferably unsalted
60 g (2 oz) dark chocolate

1. Spread a small amount of cream on the base of the dish to hold the dessert firmly. Place a layer of meringues around the edge of a dish and fill the centre with strawberries.

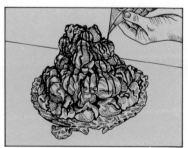

2. When all the meringues are placed to form a pyramid, from a paper cone or piping bag with a plain tube, trickle with melted butter and chocolate over the sides, using swift movements.

INGREDIENTS
6 firm eating pears

SYRUP
1 cup water
½ cup (3½ oz) sugar
1 teaspoon vanilla

FILLING
*½ cup (2½ oz) glacé fruit, finely diced, use
    any mixture you like*
1 tablespoon and 2 teaspoons brandy
*1 tablespoon and 2 teaspoons
    orange-flavoured liqueur*

STRAWBERRY CREAM
1 punnet strawberries, hulled
2 tablespoons icing sugar
2 teaspoons lemon juice
½ cup (4 fl oz) cream, whipped until stiff

PEARS IN STRAWBERRY CREAM

Peel the pears, cut them into halves. Use a melon baller or teaspoon and remove the core.

Syrup
Heat the water, sugar and vanilla in a large saucepan. Add the pears, cover and poach until they are tender, turning them over once or twice. Leave to cool in the syrup. Remove and drain well before filling.

Filling
Place the glacé fruit in a cup with brandy and orange-flavoured liqueur and leave to stand for several hours.

Fill the centre of the pear halves with this. Join halves together. Cut a little bit from the base so they will stand upright.

Strawberry Cream
Crush the strawberries with a fork on a dinner plate or in a basin. Add the icing sugar and lemon juice. Fold the strawberry mixture into the whipped cream and keep very cold.

To Serve
Place the pears on individual plates. Spoon the strawberry filling around them.

If you wish, these can have a little green leaf of angelica stuck in the top where the stalk would normally be.

Note: This fruit dish needs to be served really cold to be at its best. The pears can be filled about 12 hours before you wish to eat them but keep them covered with some plastic wrap. The strawberry cream keeps for about 4 to 5 hours.

STRAWBERRY SOUFFLÉ

This is a shortcut type of soufflé which is very easy to make provided you have an electric mixer. As the eggs in it are just beaten but not cooked, it needs lemon to freshen the flavour.

Hull the strawberries. Mash enough of them to measure one cup (8 fl oz) of pulp. You can put them in a food processor or through a sieve but be careful as a metal sieve will discolour the fruit. Make sure you have some strawberries left over to garnish the dessert.

Place the eggs and egg yolks in a bowl, beat, add the castor sugar gradually and then beat until the mixture is very thick and holds a shape. This takes about 5 to 6 minutes of beating.

Meantime mix the gelatine with the water in a cup. Stand in a small saucepan of hot water over the heat until the gelatine is clear and dissolved. Add the lemon juice to the gelatine and mix this into the strawberry pulp. Add the pulp to the egg mixture.

Whip the cream until it holds stiff peaks and fold this gently into the strawberries, one-third at a time. Add orange-flavoured liqueur. Because this mixture looks really pale and a bit uninteresting in colour, add just a couple of drops of pink food colouring to tint it.

It can be put in a bowl to chill but probably looks most attractive in a soufflé dish.

The dish should be one which holds only about 5 cups (2 pints) so that the mixture will come well above the edge. Prepare the dish with some foil to come above the edge. If you oil the band of foil with some vegetable oil it makes it easier when you remove this. Place the mixture into the dish.

Place in the refrigerator to chill. It will set in about 2 hours.

Garnish

Pipe some rosettes of cream around the edge and place some whole strawberries on the cream.

Notes: The soufflé will keep for 24 to 36 hours. There is not much gelatine in it so it won't become too firm. However, cover the top lightly with foil or plastic once it is set so it won't go hard on the surface.

When you make this soufflé, taste it and if you find it a bit eggy in flavour, you can add a little more lemon.

INGREDIENTS
2 punnets strawberries (500 g or 1 lb)
2 eggs
3 egg yolks
7 tablespoons castor sugar
1 tablespoon and 2 teaspoons gelatine
¼ cup (2 fl oz) water
3 tablespoons lemon juice
1 cup (8 fl oz) cream
2 tablespoons orange-flavoured liqueur
couple of drops of pink food colouring

GARNISH
½ cup (4 fl oz) cream, stiffly whipped
the extra strawberries

BANANAS BAKED IN FOIL

INGREDIENTS
12 medium-sized bananas

SAUCE
½ cup (5 oz) apricot jam
⅓ cup (2½ oz) orange juice
rind of 1 orange, finely grated
½ teaspoon cinnamon
1 tablespoon lemon juice
¼ cup (2 fl oz) orange-flavoured liqueur
1 tablespoon brandy

It is important when making this dish that the packages are well sealed so that all the syrup doesn't spill out on to the dish.

Place the apricot jam in a saucepan. If it is very lumpy with fruit you need to sieve it. Add the orange juice, rind, cinnamon, lemon juice, orange-flavoured liqueur and brandy and warm for a few minutes until well blended.

Peel the bananas.

Cut 6 squares of foil about 23 cm (9 in) by 23 cm (9 in).

Place 2 bananas in the centre of each square. Pull up the corners to make a box. Divide the syrup between the 6 packages. Then fold the top over tightly to enclose. Place in a moderate oven 180-190° C (350-375° F) for about 15 to 20 minutes until the bananas are soft and cooked.

Serve them in the foil packages and each person unwraps his or her own. Be careful because the heat stays inside the foil for some time.

Serve a small dish of vanilla ice cream on the side.

1. Place two bananas in the centre of a 23 cm foil square.

2. Pinch the foil firmly together at the base to seal.

3. Then press the sides of the foil together to form a package.

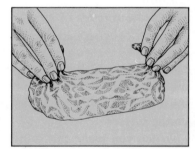

4. Put some of the syrup into each package and fold the top over to seal.

PINEAPPLE WITH ALMONDS

A very simply made dessert of fresh pineapple or if you want to make it quickly, use tinned pineapple. If using fresh, the pineapple must be quite ripe. This is good with vanilla ice cream.

If using fresh pineapple, cut into halves and remove the core. If using tinned, drain well and cut into halves or leave whole.

Heat the butter in a frying pan large enough to fit the pineapple slices in one layer. Add the sugar and cook until foaming. Then add the pineapple and cook on both sides for a couple of minutes. Remove the pineapple to a plate.

Add to the pan the rum, the Tia Maria and the brandy and cook until the sauce is syrupy. Return the pineapple and heat again. Just before serving add the almonds to the sauce.

Notes: If you wish, the dish can be partly prepared beforehand. Make it up to where you cook the sauce until syrupy. Then reheat, adding pineapple.

When cooking pineapple it becomes very acidic if you overcook so only heat until glazed.

INGREDIENTS
6 slices pineapple
45 g (1½ oz) unsalted butter
2 tablespoons sugar
⅓ cup (2½ fl oz) rum
¼ cup (2 fl oz) Tia Maria
¼ cup (2 fl oz) brandy
2 tablespoons slivered almonds, lightly
*   toasted until golden*

SPICED FRUITS

This dish can be served with cream or ice cream but the mixture is also very good inside crêpes.

Peel the pears and core them. Cut into thin slices. Melt the butter in a saucepan, add the sugar and place the pears in this. Cook with a lid on the pan, stirring or shaking for the first few minutes so that they don't brown. There should be enough natural liquid in the pears to form a syrup. If they appear to be sticking you can add a tablespoon of water.

When the pears are quite soft, add to the pan the grated orange rind, fruit mince, brandy and cinnamon. Warm until these are all heated through.

Notes: The fruit mince which can be bought in jars or tins is quite adequate. Naturally the better quality fruit mince gives a nicer dessert.

The mixture can be reheated most successfully and keeps well for about 3 or 4 days in the refrigerator, covered.

INGREDIENTS
3 eating pears, firm but not rock hard
30 g (1 oz) unsalted butter
1 tablespoon white sugar
rind of 1 orange, grated
¾ cup (7 oz) fruit mince (mincemeat)
⅓ cup (2½ oz) brandy
pinch cinnamon

ORANGE ALMOND CRÊPES

Makes 18 small crêpes.

INGREDIENTS
CRÊPES

½ cup (2 oz) flour
pinch salt
3 eggs
¼ cup (2 fl oz) brandy
½ cup (4 fl oz) milk
30 g (1 oz) melted butter

FILLING

90 g (3 oz) unsalted butter
½ cup (3½ oz) castor sugar
1 egg
1 egg yolk
60 g (2 oz) almonds, ground
1 tablespoon brandy
rind of 1 large orange, grated
extra butter

ORANGE SAUCE

90 g (3 oz) unsalted butter
4 tablespoons castor sugar
rind of 2 oranges, grated
juice of 2 oranges
3 tablespoons brandy
3 tablespoons Grand Marnier

A hot crêpe dish with an orange and almond filling which is served with an orange sauce.

Sift the flour and salt into a bowl. Make a well in the centre. Beat the eggs and add to the centre. Stir to gradually incorporate the flour. Add the brandy and milk and mix but don't overbeat as this toughens crêpes. The butter is added last.

Leave to stand for about 1 hour for the batter to rest and if it thickens too much, add a little more milk. It should be the consistency of a thin cream.

To Cook
Heat the crêpe pan first; for dessert crêpes the ideal size is about 15 cm (6 in). Add a little butter to the pan, it should sizzle and melt instantly on contact. If it doesn't then the pan isn't hot enough. Add just enough batter to the pan to coat the base, the quantity depends on the size of the pan. As you pour in the batter, tilt the pan rapidly, turning in all directions so the base is coated as quickly as possible. Place back on the heat. The surface of the crêpe will become firm and the edges will start to lift when it is cooked. Turn gently with a spatula and cook on the other side for about 15 to 20 seconds. The crêpes can be stacked on top of each other for some time and they won't stick.

Notes: This batter has a lot of eggs but they make it very light to eat. The crêpes can be made and kept for 24 hours in the refrigerator, separated by wax paper. Wrap the stack of crêpes in plastic wrap or foil. They can also be frozen, separated with wax paper and wrapped well. Leave at room temperature for a short time until thawed so you can separate them easily when you are ready to fill them.

Filling
Cream the butter and sugar until light and fluffy and then add egg and egg yolk. Mix in the almonds with the brandy and orange rind. Place a spoonful of this on one side of the crêpe and roll over, tucking the ends in well. Place them in a buttered shallow ovenproof dish in one layer.

Melt a little extra butter and brush over the top of each crêpe so they can be reheated. Leave covered in the refrigerator until you are ready to cook them. Heat uncovered in a moderate oven 180-190° C (350-375° F) for about 15 minutes.

Serve with cream or with Orange Sauce.

Orange Sauce
Melt the butter in a frying pan and add the sugar. Cook a few minutes until the mixture is foaming and looks slightly granulated but don't let the sugar brown.

Add orange rind and juice and stir until smooth. Cook until slightly thick. Remove from the heat, add brandy and Grand Marnier. Serve a spoonful over the crêpes and then the rest can be served on the table in a jug.

Notes: This makes a generous quantity of sauce but any over can be kept refrigerated for days. It is better to have plenty than to have a miserable little amount of sauce with crêpes as so often seems to happen in restaurants.

This crêpe dish is a good one to prepare beforehand. The crêpes can be completely finished and kept refrigerated for 24 hours as long as they are well covered. The sauce also can be made the day before and then reheated.

CARAMEL SAUCE

Caramel Sauce can be kept and reheated most successfully. Keep in a screw-top jar in the refrigerator. It will probably keep about two weeks.

Melt the butter and add the brown sugar. Cook until the mixture is bubbling, stirring constantly. Then add the cream and leave to cook gently until it has thickened. This may take from 10 to 15 minutes. It should coat the back of a spoon.

Remove from the heat, add brandy and vanilla. Cool and store until required.

Note: Sometimes if you overcook this and make it too thick it can become very firm and sticky. Just thin with a little extra cream when you reheat it.

INGREDIENTS
90 g (3 oz) butter
1 cup (5 oz) soft brown sugar
¾ cup (6 fl oz) cream
1 tablespoon brandy
½ teaspoon vanilla

CITRUS SOUFFLÉ

INGREDIENTS
SOUFFLÉ MIXTURE
¾ cup (6 fl oz) milk
5 tablespoons sugar
60 g (2 oz) butter
3 tablespoons flour
rind of 1 lemon, grated
rind of 1 orange, grated
⅓ cup (2½ fl oz) orange juice
¼ cup (2 fl oz) lemon juice
4 egg yolks
6 egg whites
pinch salt
pinch Cream of Tartar

ORANGE LIQUEUR SAUCE
1 egg
2 egg yolks
4 tablespoons sugar
rind of 1 lemon, grated
rind of 1 orange, grated
2 tablespoons orange liqueur
½ cup (4 fl oz) cream, whipped until stiff

The French word 'soufflé' really means 'puffed'. The base is a light sauce or purée which has stiffly beaten egg whites folded into it. Soufflés still have a reputation as kitchen troublemakers which is a pity because they are really very simple to make.

This one has a flavour of both lemon and orange, and goes well with Orange Cream (p. 134) or Orange Liqueur Sauce.

Preparation of the Soufflé Dish
So that this mixture will come well above the edge, use a soufflé dish which holds about 5 cups (2 pints). Butter the dish so the soufflé will slide up easily. Sprinkle with a little castor sugar. Tilt so that the sugar sticks to the butter and then tip out the excess.

Use a sheet of foil which will encircle the dish at least 1½ times. Fold it over lengthwise. Brush one side of the foil with butter and then place this around the dish, buttered side in with the collar well above the side of the dish. Tie with string and make sure the string is close to the top of the dish.

Place the milk and sugar in a small saucepan and warm until the sugar is dissolved.

In a separate saucepan melt the butter. Add the flour, stirring for a few minutes to cook. Remove this from the heat and stir for a moment to cool the pan. Add the milk and sugar, return to the heat and cook, stirring constantly until the mixture has thickened. It will be very thick at this stage. Add lemon rind, orange rind, orange juice and lemon juice. Mix well. Add the yolks one at a time to the hot sauce, beating them in. Leave the mixture aside to cool a little.

Place the egg whites and salt in a large bowl. Make sure that bowl and beaters are absolutely dry or the whites will not stiffen. Egg whites at room temperature will beat up to a greater volume than chilled ones. You can use an electric mixer but be careful not to overbeat. The egg white must just hold a stiff peak on the end of the beater. A large whisk and a copper bowl are ideal, if not, whip in pottery or china with electric beater or by hand. Add a little pinch of Cream of Tartar for each egg white, which helps to stabilise them.

As soon as the egg whites are stiff, add one-third of them to the warm base of lemon and orange. Then return the main mixture to the large bowl in which you've beaten the egg whites, tipping them down one side. Fold with a spatula until it is blended. It doesn't matter if there are just a few specks of egg white in the mixture.

Tip gently into the prepared soufflé dish. Place into the centre of a moderate oven 180-190° C (350-375° F) and cook for about 25 minutes to 30 minutes until it is golden and firm to touch on top. Don't open the oven before 25 minutes.

It must be cooked sufficiently to ensure that when you remove the foil collar the soufflé will stay up. However a dessert soufflé can be soft and creamy in the centre and it is nicer if it is not too firm.

When you remove the soufflé from the oven, dust the top

with some icing sugar and then remove the foil collar.

Serve immediately. It is usually easier to take the soufflé to the table on a round tray or large platter so you won't knock the sides and spoil the effect.

Notes: The orange and lemon base can be made during the day and left to cool. Keep it covered so that a skin doesn't form on the top. You can't add egg whites to a firm cold base however, so while the egg whites are being beaten, warm the orange and lemon base gently on a low heat, stirring it occasionally until it is tepid.

Orange Liqueur Sauce
This sauce is served cold with the soufflé. It is quite sweet, but then the soufflé is rather tart so they combine well.

Place the egg and yolks in a basin. Add the sugar, lemon and orange rind and orange liqueur. Beat for a minute until frothy.

Stand the basin over or in a saucepan of hot water. Keep the water hot and beat the mixture until it is thick and frothy. It will thicken and become pale in colour. This usually takes about 15 minutes. It is much easier if you have a hand-held electric beater otherwise a hand beater will do. You don't have to beat continuously, in fact until the mixture becomes tepid it is really pointless to do so.

When thick, remove and leave to cool, stirring once or twice. Fold the cream through and chill.

Notes: This is rather like making a Sabayon Sauce or Zabaglione. If you find that after keeping this, a little liquid has formed on the base of the sauce, it means that it wasn't cooked quite long enough. If this should happen, just remove all the top part and discard the liquid. It will still taste perfect.

FROZEN CANTELOUPE MOUSSE

INGREDIENTS
½ cup (4 fl oz) water
1¼ cups (9½ oz) sugar
1½ cups (12 fl oz) canteloupe purée (about
*   1 medium-sized canteloupe)*
2 tablespoons lemon juice
¼ cup (2 fl oz) cream

In France you can buy tiny perfumed *charentais* melons which are used for this recipe, but one of our ripe canteloupes makes a very good mousse. You must buy one that is really ripe and perfumed however, as a firm, tasteless canteloupe makes a really tasteless mousse.

You can serve the mousse in little canteloupe shells, or place on plates and then arrange a couple of wedges of cold canteloupe around this. It is very refreshing on a hot day, or after any rich meal.

Place the water and sugar in a saucepan and heat gently until the sugar is dissolved. Then turn up the heat so that the mixture is just gently bubbling and cook for about 5 minutes or until it looks slightly syrupy. Cool to tepid.

You can put the canteloupe flesh in a food processor or push it through a coarse sieve. Don't use the firm part right next to the skin of the fruit. Add the juice of the lemon to the canteloupe.

Mix the sugar syrup into the canteloupe and then stir in the cream. Place into a metal tray to freeze. When frozen it will be rather icy. Remove from the freezer, place into a bowl and beat really well until it forms a thick mush. Return to the freezer. When it freezes this time it should be slightly softer, without any icy granules. Cover after it has firmed.

Serve directly from the freezer.

Note: This can be kept for a week, although it is nicest if eaten within about 3 to 4 days.

FROZEN STRAWBERRY MOUSSE

INGREDIENTS
⅔ cup (5¼ oz) sugar
½ cup (4 fl oz) water
500 g (1 lb) ripe strawberries (2 punnets,
*   approximately)*
2 tablespoons lemon juice
½ cup (4 fl oz) cream

One of the loveliest of all frozen desserts, this mousse can be either served on its own or accompanied by some whole fresh strawberries or raspberries.

Place the sugar and water in a saucepan and heat gently until the sugar is dissolved. Turn up the heat so the mixture is just gently bubbling and cook for about 5 minutes or until it looks slightly syrupy. When ready it should measure about ¾ cup. Remove and leave to cool.

Sieve or purée the strawberries. If you sieve them be careful as aluminium discolours the fruit. Add the lemon juice and mix with the syrup. Pour into ice cream trays or a container and freeze. It will be icy and rather granulated. Remove from the freezer when firm.

Whip the cream until it holds very soft peaks. Beat the strawberry mixture until it is slightly creamy but don't let it go soft. Add the cream, folding through thoroughly and then return to the freezer. Once firm, cover the top with foil.

Serve directly from the freezer.

Note: It keeps very well for at least 7 to 10 days.

FROZEN CITRUS SOUFFLÉ

This is one of the frozen desserts which features in so many top French restaurants. Light as a feather and very fresh it can be kept for some time in the freezer. Unlike an ice cream it melts very quickly, so should be served directly from the freezer.

For the best effect put it in a container so that it comes above the edge like a soufflé. You can use a metal container but wrap a white serviette around it to take to the table.

This is first cooked in a basin or double boiler. You need to beat the mixture until it becomes light and fluffy. However you can wait until it warms a little so it is quicker, beating a cold mixture is a futile job and very slow. It is this procedure which gives the finished dish the lightness which makes it so good. Use either a hand beater, or a hand-held electric beater.

Place the egg yolks and castor sugar in a basin. Beat with a whisk until light, add the orange rind and juice, lemon rind and juice and mix. Place this basin over hot water or stand in a pan of hot water and stir for a few minutes until it has warmed. Then using your beater, beat really well until it is very thick and fluffy and holds a shape when the mixture falls back on itself.

Remove and beat a moment to cool. Add the orange liqueur and the Kirsch.

Beat the egg whites until stiff, add sugar and beat again until stiff. Fold the egg whites one-third at a time into the orange and lemon base.

Pour into a container. If you use one which is only about 3-4 cups (1¼-1½ pints) it should come well above the edge. However you need to wrap a double thickness of foil around the dish and tie with string first.

Once the soufflé is frozen then it is removed. Place the mould on a plate, wrap a serviette around it and decorate with a rosebud on the side if you want to be very French.

INGREDIENTS

6 egg yolks
½ cup (3½ oz) castor sugar
rind of 1 orange, finely grated
¼ cup (2 fl oz) orange juice
rind of 1 lemon, finely grated
¼ cup (2 fl oz) lemon juice
2 tablespoons orange-flavoured liqueur
2 tablespoons Kirsch
4 egg whites
additional ½ cup (3½ oz) castor sugar

ICE CREAM

Home-made ice cream is a real luxury and doesn't have any resemblance to the commercial variety. It is divided into various categories, cream ices and sorbets which are rather more fruity in flavour. I have tested these recipes in the average freezer and have not used any special equipment for making them, such as an ice cream churn. You must use the best quality ingredients and as some of the flavour is lost when freezing they should all be very well flavoured in the beginning.

One of the most important things to note is that home-made ice cream should be removed from your freezer and transferred to the ordinary part of the refrigerator for about 20 to 30 minutes before serving it. This allows the ice cream to soften and mellow and the improvement in both flavour and texture is tremendous.

When you make ice cream, the sugar content is important; not enough and it becomes rough and granulated, too much and it won't set properly. If you remember this, you can adjust your recipes so they are right for your freezer, as freezers vary a little. It is better to have it a little on the firm side rather than too soft, and then leave to soften in the refrigerator before serving.

STRAWBERRY ICE CREAM

INGREDIENTS
250 g (8 oz) ripe strawberries (1 punnet, approximately)
¾ cup (5 oz) castor sugar
1 tablespoon lemon juice
1 cup (8 fl oz) thick or pure cream

I have included this because it is so quick and easy and yet really captures the fresh taste and aroma of strawberries. It is only worth making when strawberries are in season, as hot-house fruit makes a very poor and acidic ice cream.

Hull the strawberries and then mash them into a pulp or put them in a food processor. You should have just on one cup (8 fl oz) of purée.

Add the castor sugar and stir until it has almost dissolved. Add the lemon juice. Whip the cream until it holds soft peaks.

Fold the strawberry mixture into the cream. Place it into an ice cream container. Leave until it has partly frozen around the edges, then take a fork and stir it really well. Freeze until solid and cover with foil.

About 20 minutes before serving remove from the freezer and place in the ordinary part of the refrigerator for the ice cream to mellow.

Note: If you wish, you can add a little orange-flavoured liqueur to the ice cream mixture; be careful, though, not to lose any of the fresh fruit taste.

NESSELRODE ICE CREAM

This makes quite a large quantity which freezes well. Based on a custard, chestnut purée forms the main texture as a background to the fruits. The chestnut purée can be bought in most large shops or delicatessens. Be certain to buy the unsweetened, usually marked 'Nature' purée.

Fruit

Place the sultanas in a cup or small bowl. Chop the cherries into quarters and add with the peel. Press the mixture down lightly and add enough brandy to come level with the top of the fruit. Leave to stand for 1 hour.

Ice Cream

Beat the egg yolks and castor sugar in a basin until light. Place the cream and milk in a saucepan and heat until it is just boiling. Remove the pan, tip the hot cream and milk into the eggs, stirring constantly. Then return the mixture to the pan and whisk constantly until it is lightly thickened. Be careful not to let it boil. If it seems to be getting too hot, lift from the heat and whisk for a moment. A double boiler could be used but is tedious and slow.

Remove the saucepan from the heat. Cut the chestnut purée which is a rather solid mixture, into about 6 pieces. Add these to the custard and stir until the purée has melted. Add the brandy-soaked fruits and vanilla and leave to cool.

Mix the castor sugar into the cream and whisk to stiffen slightly. Fold into the chestnut custard.

Place in a basin or container to freeze. If the custard is a bit on the thin side, the fruit will all sink to the bottom, so as it freezes and firms up, stir once or twice so it is evenly distributed.

When frozen, cover the top with foil. Before serving, remove the ice cream to the ordinary part of the refrigerator for about 20 minutes to improve the texture. It can be turned out and decorated if you wish.

Serve with warm Caramel Sauce (p. 141)

INGREDIENTS
Makes about 4 cups of mixture.

FRUIT
½ cup (3 oz) sultanas
¼ cup (1½ oz) glacé cherries
¼ cup (1½ oz) mixed peel
brandy

ICE CREAM
5 egg yolks
1 cup (7 oz) castor sugar
1 cup (8 fl oz) cream
1 cup (8 fl oz) milk
1 tin unsweetened chestnut purée
   (size 440 g [1 lb])
1 teaspoon vanilla
3 tablespoons castor sugar
additional 1 cup (8 fl oz) cream, whipped
   until it holds peaks

CHESTNUT CAKE

INGREDIENTS

CAKE

3 egg yolks
5 tablespoons castor sugar
1 teaspoon vanilla essence
½ cup (2 oz) plain flour
¼ cup (1 oz) cornflour
1 teaspoon baking powder
3 egg whites

CHESTNUT FILLING

1 tin unsweetened chestnut purée
   (size 440 g [1 lb])
7 tablespoons icing sugar
4 tablespoons brandy
¾ cup (6 fl oz) cream, whipped until stiff

TO FINISH

90 g (3 oz) dark chocolate

Beat the egg yolks with castor sugar until very thick. It is easiest if done with an electric mixer. Add vanilla essence, mix in.

Sift the plain flour, cornflour and baking powder together twice. Beat the egg whites until they hold stiff peaks. Add the flour and egg white alternately to the yolk and sugar mixture. It is a rather stiff consistency when finished.

You can make this in either a 23 cm (9 in) round or square tin. Butter the tin, line the base with a piece of greaseproof paper and brush this with butter. Pour the mixture into the tin and bake in a moderate oven 180-190° C (350-375° F) for about 25 minutes or until it is just firm to touch on top and it has shrunk away slightly from the sides. Remove and leave to cool for 5 minutes. Turn out onto a cake rack.

Chestnut Filling

Mash the chestnut purée using a fork or a mixer. Be certain that you always use unsweetened purée which is usually labelled 'Nature', as the sweetened will be far too sickly.

Add the icing sugar gradually and then the brandy. Fold the whipped cream through the mixture.

To Assemble

Place the cake on a bench and cut into three slices, using a serrated knife. Place one slice of cake down, cover with a layer of the chestnut cream, then place another layer of cake on top, then more chestnut cream and finish with cake. Use about 3 or 4 tablespoons of the chestnut cream each time. Cover the sides of the cake with chestnut cream but keep about ½ cup (4 fl oz) aside for decorating. Chill this ½ cup of cream.

To Finish

Place the chocolate, broken into squares, in a small basin. Stand in a pan of water and heat until the chocolate is melted, stirring occasionally. It should be smooth and glossy.

Spread this chocolate over the top of the cake. Chill until the chocolate is set.

Take the remaining ½ cup (4 fl oz) chestnut cream which was left aside and put into a piping bag with a star tube. Pipe little rosettes around the edge of the chocolate on top. Then chill the cake again.

Serve a bowl of whipped cream separately with this cake.

Notes: The cake is nicest if made about 10 hours before eating so the flavours mature. It keeps for 2 or 3 days.

COFFEE HAZELNUT TORTE

For the base of this dessert make up one of the sponge recipes as in Dessert Cake with Chocolate Cream and Strawberries (p.152). Make it in a square tin, 23 cm (9 in) diameter. If you bake the cake the day before it is easier to handle. Cut into halves through the centre, using a serrated knife.

Chop the hazelnuts very finely or grind or mince them. Place on a baking tray in the oven until golden, or you can put them in a dry frying pan and heat until golden. Stir occasionally.

Divide the nut mixture into halves, one half will go in the filling, the other on the outside of the cake.

Place the icing sugar and butter in a mixing bowl and cream until very light and fluffy. Mix the instant coffee and boiling water together and add them gradually to the butter. Beat in the egg. Be careful the mixture doesn't curdle or the texture is spoilt. If it should curdle, stand the bowl for a few minutes in some warm water and beat with a wooden spoon. Lastly fold in the whipped cream and half the hazelnuts. When firm cover with plastic wrap.

To Assemble

Mix the brandy or rum and milk together. Place one half of the cake on a bench. Brush the surface with some of the brandy or rum and milk. Spread the coffee and hazelnut filling over this. Then brush one surface of the other slice of cake with the milk mixture and place this side down over the filling. Press firmly. Chill until set.

To Finish

Whip the cream until it holds soft peaks. Add the icing sugar and brandy or rum. Spread this over the top and sides of the cake. Press hazelnuts all over the sides. The easiest way to do this is to place wax paper, cut into triangles, under the cake. The triangles have their points towards the centre, then the cake is placed on this. As the hazelnuts fall onto the paper you then gently pull the paper out. Keep chilled.

Notes: The cake can be made several days before eating but coat with cream on the day you are going to serve it.

If you wish to remove the skins from the hazelnuts before toasting them, place the whole hazelnuts on a baking tray and place in a moderate oven for about 15 minutes until the skins loosen. Place them in a tea towel and rub firmly. Most of the skins will come away. You then chop and toast as you wish.

INGREDIENTS

FILLING

100 g (3½ oz approx) hazelnuts
½ cup (2½ oz) icing sugar
125 g (4 oz) unsalted butter
1 tablespoon instant coffee
1 tablespoon boiling water
1 egg
1 tablespoon cream, lightly whipped

TO ASSEMBLE

¼ cup (2 fl oz) brandy or rum (use same flavouring as To Finish above)
¼ cup (2 fl oz) milk

TO FINISH

1 cup (8 fl oz) cream
2 tablespoons icing sugar
1 tablespoon brandy or rum
the remainder of the toasted hazelnuts

FRENCH CHOCOLATE CAKE

This chocolate cake needs to be removed from the oven while it is still slightly soft and then it firms up as it cools. It is beautifully rich and very moist.

INGREDIENTS

INGREDIENTS
125 g (4 oz) butter
¾ cup (5 oz) castor sugar
3 egg yolks
125 g (4 oz) dark chocolate
45 g (1½ oz) ground almonds
3 egg whites
1 tablespoon castor sugar
½ cup (2 oz) plain flour

TO DECORATE
1 cup (8 fl oz) cream
1 tablespoon castor sugar
½ teaspoon vanilla

FOR MEDALLIONS
60 g (2 oz) dark chocolate

Butter a square or round tin 20 cm (8 in) in size. Then line the base with some greaseproof paper. Butter this again.

Cream the butter with the castor sugar until light and fluffy. Add the egg yolks one at a time.

Place the chocolate, broken into sections, in a small bowl and stand this in a pan of water. Heat, mixing occasionally until the chocolate is smooth and glossy. Remove. Leave until it has cooled and is just tepid. Add the chocolate to the butter with the ground almonds.

Beat the egg whites until they are very stiff. Add the tablespoon of castor sugar and beat again. Sift the flour. Mix the egg whites and flour alternately into the chocolate mixture. The chocolate is rather stiff so you need to fold fairly firmly, but use a spatula and fold from the bottom to the top, turning the bowl as you go. Place into the prepared tin.

Bake in a moderate oven 180-190° C (350-375° F) until firm on top, it usually takes about 25 minutes. If you put a thin skewer into the centre this should come out moist. Remove and leave to cool in the tin. Turn out.

Because the cake is rather rich it is best covered with cream for serving. Don't ice it as this makes it too sweet.

To Decorate

Whip the cream until it holds soft peaks. Add the sugar and vanilla and beat again for a moment until stiff. Cover the top and sides of the cake with the cream. You can pipe some rosettes on top if you wish, using a star tube.

Chocolate Medallions

Place the chocolate, broken into small pieces, into a small bowl. Stand this in a pan with a little water and stand over the heat, stirring until the chocolate has melted and is glossy.

Place a piece of wax paper down on a board. Using the back of a teaspoon form tiny circles of the chocolate on the paper. Place the board in a cool place or in the refrigerator until they have set. They peel away from the paper easily. They can be stored in the refrigerator or a cool cupboard and won't melt unless the weather is hot. Place them either on the top of the cake or around the sides.

Note: The cake is nicest if eaten within 48 hours of making it.

WALNUT CAKE WITH LEMON SYRUP

This walnut cake is a little like a Greek cake because it is soaked in a lemon and rum syrup. It is nicest eaten within 36 hours of making as the flavour in the syrup tends to disappear.

Mix the nuts together with the biscuits and lemon rind. Place the egg yolks in a mixing bowl and add the sugar. Beat until quite light and pale.

Separately beat the egg whites until stiff. Fold the whites into the yolks, one-third at a time. Then put the nuts to one side of the mixture. Gently fold them through. The mixture will look rather soft and sticky once you add the nuts.

This can be cooked in a sponge tin or square tin about 20 cm (8 in) in size. Butter the tin. I have found that the cake can be difficult to turn out and, as it becomes wet with the syrup, can stick. It is much easier to handle if you place a piece of foil on the base and butter this. Pour mixture into the tin. Bake in a moderate oven, 180-190° C (350-375° F) until just firm on top, it usually takes about 20 to 25 minutes.

Remove and while warm poke some holes, with a fine skewer, all over the cake. Pour the syrup over.

Syrup

Make the syrup while the cake is cooking. Boil the water, sugar, lemon juice and cinnamon for about 5 minutes or until it is slightly syrupy. Add the rum. Leave aside.

The syrup is poured over the cake whilst hot. At first it appears that all the syrup won't go in so you need to just pour it over gradually.

Leave the cake to cool in the tin. When cold turn out on to a plate. It will be soft and slightly sticky. If you wish you can cover the top with some cream.

Cream

Whip the cream until it holds soft peaks, add vanilla and castor sugar and whip again for a minute. Spread this over the top of the cake.

INGREDIENTS

CAKE
¾ cup (3 oz) walnuts, finely ground
¾ cup (3 oz) almonds, finely ground
4 plain biscuits, finely crushed
rind of 2 lemons, grated
3 egg yolks
⅓ cup (2¼ oz) sugar
3 egg whites

SYRUP
¾ cup (6 fl oz) water
½ cup (3½ oz) sugar
3 tablespoons lemon juice
¼ teaspoon cinnamon
3 tablespoons brown rum

CREAM
1 cup cream
½ teaspoon vanilla essence
1 tablespoon castor sugar

DESSERT CAKE WITH CHOCOLATE CREAM AND STRAWBERRIES

INGREDIENTS

3 eggs
½ cup (3½ oz) castor sugar
⅔ cup (3½ oz) flour
pinch of salt

CHOCOLATE FILLING

90 g (3 oz) dark chocolate, broken into
  squares
1 cup (8 fl oz) cream
2 punnets strawberries

CHOCOLATE GLAZE AND DECORATION

30 g (1 oz) unsalted butter
185 g (6 oz) dark chocolate
½ cup (4 fl oz) cream, whipped until it
  holds stiff peaks
the strawberries which are remaining from
  the cake

This is not really complicated but more a matter of assembling all the various ingredients. It is a sponge which is layered with chocolate cream and whole strawberries and then coated with chocolate and left to set.

Sponge
If you have a recipe for a sponge which you make easily you can use that. It needs to be made in a square tin for the cake to be assembled easily. This particular sponge is very light and is best made the day before so that it cuts easily.

This sponge is best made with an electric mixer. Place the eggs and castor sugar into the mixer and beat until the mixture is so thick that it leaves a ribbon on itself when the beaters are lifted.
   Sift the flour and salt, twice. Fold very gently into the eggs.
   Butter a square 20 cm (8 in) tin and line the base with a square of greaseproof paper. Butter this too. Place the sponge mixture evenly into the tin.
   Bake in a moderate oven 180-190° C (350-375° F) for about 20 minutes or until just firm to touch on top. When it has cooled for about 5 minutes, turn out on to a wire rack.

Chocolate Filling
Place the chocolate into a small basin and stand it over or in a saucepan of hot water and heat until warm. Stir until melted and glossy smooth. Remove to cool a few minutes.
   Add the cream to the chocolate. If you add the chocolate to the cold cream it tends to go into thready pieces, so put it in the bowl in which you melted the chocolate, stir to get all the little bits from the sides and then remove to a cold basin. Refrigerate until quite cold, about 1 hour.
   Use a whisk to whip lightly so it just holds a very soft shape.
   Hull the strawberries and keep chilled.

To Assemble
Cut the sponge into three layers across. Cut 2 of these layers into halves and then the third layer into halves and across. Place the larger strips of cake in the base and on the sides of a log tin, 20 cm (8 in) by about 10 cm (4 in) in size. Put the two shorter pieces on the ends. Spoon a thin layer of the chocolate filling over the base of the cake. Then arrange a layer of strawberries very close together on top of the chocolate, spoon a little more chocolate over the strawberries. Then place another piece of sponge on this, more cream, strawberries, more chocolate, and top with the remaining piece of cake. (You will probably have some strawberries over which you can use for garnish.) Press down gently to make sure there won't be any air gaps. If the cake on the edges is uneven with the top of the tin, carefully level this. Cover with plastic wrap. Chill for about 6 to 8 hours.
   Turn out, it will come out easily and be quite firm.

Chocolate Glaze and Decoration

Place the butter in a small saucepan and heat until foaming. Break the chocolate into small pieces. Add to the butter, remove immediately from the heat and stir until it is melted. There should be sufficient heat in the saucepan to melt this, you can return to the heat if there isn't but be careful not to make the chocolate hot.

Using a spatula, spread a thin layer of the chocolate over the top and sides of the cake. It will appear to soak in. Leave for a minute, this holds any crumbs flat. Then coat with another layer of chocolate. Place any remaining chocolate in a paper cone and cut a small end. Decorate the top with a pattern.

Chill for about 30 minutes to set the chocolate. Pipe some rosettes around the edge and then decorate with the remaining strawberries. Keep chilled.

Note: It keeps successfully for 24 hours.

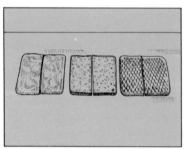

1. Cut the sponge through into three layers. Cut them through as shown, cutting one outside section of the cake in two pieces, the other outside section in half and them across on one side. Cut inside portion just in two. Line base and sides of square tin, placing outside of the cake against the tin, as this makes a smoother surface for coating with chocolate.

2. When log cake is coated smoothly with chocolate, pipe a lattice or decoration over the top.

EQUIVALENT TERMS

Most culinary terms in the English-speaking world can cross national borders without creating havoc in the kitchen. Nevertheless, local usage can produce some problems. The following list contains names of ingredients, equipment and cookery terms that are used in this book, but which may not be familiar to all readers.

USED IN THIS BOOK	ALSO KNOWN AS
baking powder	double-acting baking powder
baking tray	baking sheet
Belgian endive	whitlof/chickory
bicarbonate of soda	baking soda
biscuits	cookies
blender	liquidiser
boiler chicken	stewing chicken
pepper, red or green	sweet or bell pepper, capsicum
castor sugar	fine granulated sugar, super-fine sugar
cod	groper
cornflour	cornstarch
crayfish	crawfish
dark chocolate	semi-sweet chocolate
desiccated coconut	shredded coconut
essence	extract
eggplant	aubergine
fillet (of meat)	tenderloin
frying pan	skillet
glacé (fruits)	candied
green beans	runner beans
grill/griller	broil/broiler
hard boiled egg	hard-cooked egg
haricot beans	white beans
icing sugar	confectioners' sugar
log tin	tube pan
minced	ground
mincer	grinder
okra	gumbo, ladies' fingers
pastry	pie crust
pinch (of salt)	dash
plain flour	all-purpose flour
rosewater essence	rose extract
scone tray	biscuit tray
self-raising flour	self-rising flour
sieve	strain/strainer
(to) sift	(to) strain
snapper (fish)	sea bass
spring onions	scallions, green onions
stone, seed, pip	pit
Swiss roll tin	jelly roll pan
tea towel	dish towel, glass cloth
(to) whisk	(to) whip, beat
zucchini	courgettes

GUIDE TO WEIGHT AND MEASURES

When following the recipes in this book, a good set of scales, a graduated measuring cup and a set of measuring spoons will be very helpful and can be obtained from leading hardware and kitchenware stores.

All cup and spoon measurements are level:

The measuring cup has a capacity of 250 millilitres (250 ml).

The tablespoon has a capacity of 20 millilitres (20 ml).

The teaspoon has a capacity of 5 millilitres (5 ml).

In all recipes, imperial equivalents of metric measures are shown in parentheses, e.g. 500 g (1 lb) beef. Although the metric yields of cup and weighed measures are approximately 10 per cent greater than the imperial yields, the proportions remain the same. Therefore, for successful cooking use either metric or imperial weights and measures — do not mix the two.

New Zealand, British, United States and Canadian weights and measures are the same as Australian weights and measures except that:

(a) the Australian and British Standard tablespoons have a capacity of 20 millilitres (20 ml) whereas the New Zealand, United States and Canadian Standard tablespoons have a capacity of 15 millilitres (15 ml), therefore all tablespoon measures should be taken generously in those countries;

(b) the imperial pint (Australia, New Zealand and Britain) has a capacity of 20 fl oz whereas the US pint used in the United States and Canada has a capacity of 16 fl oz, therefore pint measures should be increased accordingly in those two countries.

The following charts of conversion equivalents will be useful:

IMPERIAL & METRIC WEIGHT

Imperial Weight	Metric Weight	Imperial Liquid Measures	Cup Measures	Metric Liquid Measures
½ oz	15g			
1 oz	30 g	1 fl oz		30 ml
2 oz	60 g	2 fl oz	¼ cup	
3 oz	90 g	3 fl oz		100 ml
4 oz (¼ lb)	125 g	4 fl oz (¼ pint US)	½ cup	
6 oz	185 g	5 fl oz (¼ pint imp)		150 ml
8 oz (½ lb)	250 g	6 fl oz	¾ cup	
12 oz (¾ lb)	375 g	8 fl oz (½ pint US)	1 cup	250 ml
16 oz (1 lb)	500 g	10 fl oz (½ pint imp)	1¼ cups	
24 oz (1½ lb)	750 g	12 fl oz	1½ cups	
32 oz (2 lb)	1000 g (1 kg)	14 fl oz	1¾ cups	
3 lb	1500 g (1.5 kg)	16 fl oz (1 pint US)	2 cups	500 ml
4 lb	2000 g (2 kg)	20 fl oz (1 pint imp)	2½ cups	
		32 fl oz	4 cups	1 litre

Key: oz = ounce; lb = pound; g = gram; kg = kilogram

Key: fl oz = fluid ounce; ml = millilitre

OVEN TEMPERATURE GUIDE

The Celsius and Fahrenheit temperatures in the chart below relate to most gas ovens. Increase by 20° C or 50° F for electric ovens or refer to the manufacturer's temperature guide. For temperatures below 160° C (325° F), do not increase the given temperature.

Description of oven	Celsius ° C	Fahrenheit ° F	Gas Mark
Cool	100	200	¼
Very Slow	120	250	½
Slow	150	300	2
Moderately Slow	160	325	3
Moderate	180	350	4
Moderately Hot	190	375	5
Hot	200	400	6
Very Hot	230	450	8

INDEX